BARRON'S BOOK NOTES

WILLIAM SHAKESPEARE'S
King Lear

BY

Arthur S. Rosenblatt

SERIES EDITOR

Michael Spring
Editor, *Literary Cavalcade*
Scholastic Inc.

BARRON'S EDUCATIONAL SERIES, INC.
Woodbury, New York / London / Toronto / Sydney

ACKNOWLEDGMENTS

We would like to thank Loreto Todd, Senior Lecturer in English, University of Leeds, England, for preparing the chapter on Elizabethan English in this book.

We would like to acknowledge the many painstaking hours of work Holly Hughes and Thomas F. Hirsch have devoted to making the *Book Notes* series a success.

All inquiries should be addressed to:
Barron's Educational Series, Inc.
113 Crossways Park Drive
Woodbury, New York 11797

Library of Congress Catalog Card No. 84-18428

International Standard Book No. 0-8120-3425-2

Library of Congress Cataloging in Publication Data
Rosenblatt, Arthur S.
   William Shakespeare's King Lear.

   (Barron's book notes)
   Bibliography: p. 100
   Summary: A guide to reading "King Lear" with a critical
and appreciative mind. Includes background on the author's
life and times, sample tests, term paper suggestions, and a
reading list.
   1. Shakespeare, William, 1564–1616. King Lear.
[1. Shakespeare, William, 1564–1616. King Lear.
2. English literature—History and criticism] I. Title.
II. Series.
PR2819.R67   1984   822.3'3   84-18428
ISBN 0-8120-3425-2 (pbk.)

PRINTED IN THE UNITED STATES OF AMERICA

456   550   98765432

CONTENTS

ADVISORY BOARD

HOW TO USE THIS BOOK

You have to know how to approach literature in order to get the most out of it. This *Barron's Book Notes* volume follows a plan based on methods used by some of the best students to read a work of literature.

Begin with the guide's section on the author's life and times. As you read, try to form a clear picture of the author's personality, circumstances, and motives for writing the work. This background usually will make it easier for you to hear the author's tone of voice, and follow where the author is heading.

Then go over the rest of the introductory material—such sections as those on the plot, characters, setting, themes, and style of the work. Underline, or write down in your notebook, particular things to watch for, such as contrasts between characters and repeated literary devices. At this point, you may want to develop a system of symbols to use in marking your text as you read. (Of course, you should only mark up a book you own, not one that belongs to another person or a school.) Perhaps you will want to use a different letter for each character's name, a different number for each major theme of the book, a different color for each important symbol or literary device. Be prepared to mark up the pages of your book as you read. Put your marks in the margins so you can find them again easily.

Now comes the moment you've been waiting for—the time to start reading the work of literature. You may want to put aside your *Barron's Book Notes* volume until you've read the work all the way through. Or you may want to alternate, reading the *Book Notes* analysis of each section as soon as you have finished reading the corresponding part of the original. Before you move on, reread crucial passages you don't fully understand. (Don't take this guide's analysis for granted—make up your own mind as to what the work means.)

Once you've finished the whole work of literature, you may want to review it right away, so you can firm up your ideas about what it means. You may want to leaf through the book concentrating on passages you marked in reference to one character or one theme. This is also a good time to reread the *Book Notes* introductory material, which pulls together insights on specific topics.

When it comes time to prepare for a test or to write a paper, you'll already have formed ideas about the work. You'll be able to go back through it, refreshing your memory as to the author's exact words and perspective, so that you can support your opinions with evidence drawn straight from the work. Patterns will emerge, and ideas will fall into place; your essay question or term paper will almost write itself. Give yourself a dry run with one of the sample tests in the guide. These tests present both multiple-choice and essay questions. An accompanying section gives answers to the multiple-choice questions as well as suggestions for writing the essays. If you have to select a term paper topic, you may choose one from the list of suggestions in this book. This guide also provides you with a reading list, to help you when you start research for a term paper, and a selection of provocative comments by critics, to spark your thinking before you write.

THE AUTHOR
AND HIS TIMES

It would be nice if we could say that William Shakespeare wrote *King Lear* when he himself was at an advanced age. We could picture him becoming concerned with retirement and the disposal of his property and goods. But the theory collapses when you realize that Shakespeare was only 41 years old when the first performance of *King Lear* was recorded in an official document.

Besides, the plot line, involving two older men and their respective family problems, is only a small part of the play. *King Lear* is about much, much more and undoubtedly reflects deeper concerns that Shakespeare had developed in his already considerable experience as a playwright.

By the time he wrote *King Lear*, this adventurous young man from Stratford had led a remarkable life, even for Elizabethan times, which we tend to think of as more exciting than our own. During the reign of Elizabeth I, England experienced a period of relative stability and, more important, prosperity. All the arts flourished, but the growth of drama was nothing short of phenomenal. At the zenith of Elizabeth's power and influence, William Shakespeare came to London and wrote the 37 plays that have established him as the greatest playwright in the English language.

How did it all begin? What purpose drove him to produce this incredible body of work? Where did his inspiration come from?

There are many theories about Shakespeare, but very little that is known for certain. He was born in

1564 and raised in Stratford-on-Avon, some 100 miles from London. His father was a successful middle-class tradesman and had even held public office. Young Will attended local schools, which means he received a good, substantial education. It gave him a background in the classics as well as proficiency in the three "Rs."

At 18, William married Anne Hathaway, eight years his senior. She subsequently bore a daughter, Susanna, and shortly afterward, twins, Hamnet and Judith.

How the young husband provided for his family during the first years of marriage is unknown. A strong tradition holds that he was employed locally as a schoolteacher, but there is no evidence to prove it.

We do know that he left Stratford sometime in his mid-20s and settled in London. There he first came to notice as a poet, the writer of two long poems, *Venus and Adonis* and *The Rape of Lucrece*. These poems were favorably received and launched his reputation.

About the same time, he turned his attention to the theater. He wrote one tragedy, *Titus Andronicus*, but most of his earliest plays were comedies, including *The Comedy of Errors*, *Two Gentlemen of Verona*, *Love's Labor's Lost*, and *The Taming of the Shrew*. Romantic comedy, satire, farce—all flowed from his pen at the outset of his career. They concerned relationships among lovers, friends, families, but they didn't plumb the depths.

Overlapping the production of these comedies were his earliest history plays. Toward the end of the 16th century Shakespeare produced the series of four great historical works that remain the pinnacle of his achievement in that type of theater—*Richard II; Henry IV, Part I; Henry IV, Part II;* and *Henry V*.

As the years wore on, Shakespeare turned from his interest in politics and the glorification of England to more profound comedies. Two of the best known, *Measure for Measure* and *All's Well that Ends Well*, show an interest in darker human behavior.

It's not surprising, then, that the greatest of Shakespeare's tragedies were also written during this period, the first decade of the new century. Now the poet-playwright was at the absolute height of his powers, and one brilliant drama followed the next—*Hamlet*, *Othello*, *King Lear*, and *Macbeth*, all written and performed within a few short years.

Shakespeare was still relatively young, but he had matured. He was a playwright of some repute, and also an actor who performed both in his own plays and in plays by others. He could very well afford to look around and question why everything in life wasn't perfect and rosy.

King Lear examines a broad range of philosophic ideas. There's a somber tone and not much frivolity in the play. But the playwright in Shakespeare knew he couldn't simply stage a dull discussion of abstract notions. And so he told a story in order to hold the audience's attention and to get his points across. The play explores more profound themes than any of Shakespeare's tragedies, but it also offers a central figure of such heroic proportion that our attention is riveted to him and his fate. When you read the play today, or see it performed, you can't help but be moved by the powerful speech Shakespeare puts into the mouths of his characters—speech so rich and poetic that some readers refer to *King Lear* as Shakespeare's greatest poem.

Shakespeare continued to write tragedies—*Coriolanus*, *Macbeth*, *Antony and Cleopatra*—but he found the world of myth a better setting for his developing interests. A new type of play, the romantic tragicomedy, began to appear—*The Winter's Tale, The Tempest, Cymbeline.*

Shakespeare's involvement with a theatrical company called the King's Men—both as actor and playwright—kept him active until 1613, when the Globe Theatre in which the company performed burned down. Perhaps he took it as an omen, but Shakespeare returned at about that time to Stratford, where he spent his final years. He died on April 23, 1616, at the age of 52.

William Shakespeare never lived to be as old as Lear. Nor was he ever a king. But his rich imagination and talent enabled him to create a world so true that we can enter it even today.

THE PLAY

The Plot

There are really two plots in *King Lear*, a main plot and a fully developed subplot. Each has its own set of characters.

In the main plot, there is the head of the family, the 80-plus-year-old king of Britain, Lear. He has three daughters, Goneril, Regan, and Cordelia. The Duke of Albany is married to the oldest, Goneril, and the Duke of Cornwall is married to Regan, the middle daughter. Cordelia has two suitors, the Duke of Burgundy and the King of France. The court jester, the Fool, is by extension a member of the Lear family and part of the main plot, as is the Earl of Kent, Lear's loyal follower.

The Earl of Gloucester, also a member of Lear's court, is the head of another family and the focus of the subplot. He has two offspring, an older, legitimate son named Edgar and a younger, illegitimate or bastard son named Edmund.

Various minor characters appear from time to time. They are easily identified by their connections with whatever main character they serve or speak of.

As the play opens, Lear has decided to retire and divide his kingdom among his three daughters. Cordelia's husband will be chosen for her immediately after Lear executes this "living will." Before he allots the shares, Lear asks each daughter to make a profession of her love for him in order to receive her entitlement. Goneril and Regan waste no time professing love for their father, but Cordelia is speechless. She loves her father as any daughter should, no more and no less. Lear is outraged by what he sees as her lack of devotion. He cuts Cordelia out of her share and banishes her. Her share is divided between Goneril and Regan. Lear gives them everything but keeps a retinue, a following of 100 knights who will accompany him as he alternates monthly visits between his two daughters. Cordelia's suitors are called in. Without a dowry, Burgundy rejects her; but the King of France sees her true worth and leads Cordelia off to marriage and his protection.

At Gloucester's castle, Edmund reveals that he will not let his illegitimate birth and older brother prevent him from inheriting his father's estate. He devises a plan to convince Gloucester that Edgar is secretly planning to kill his father to get his hands on the family property and enjoy it while he's still young. Edmund then tells Edgar that their father is after him for some mistaken notion of a reported crime. Eventually Gloucester is convinced of Edgar's treachery and seeks to put his older son to death. Edgar flees for his life.

Meanwhile, Lear discovers that living with his two daughters is no joy. He is so outraged by their cruel behavior toward him that he curses them and rushes out into a violent storm. During his exposure to the elements he is accompanied by Kent, the Fool (his court jester), and eventually by Edgar, who has disguised himself as a lunatic beggar named "poor Tom."

Gloucester tries to help Lear and his followers but is betrayed to Cornwall and Regan by Edmund. As punishment, Gloucester is blinded and sent out into the storm, too. Edgar, still disguised, discovers his blind father and leads him to Dover, where he joins Lear, who has gone mad from exposure to the elements and the anguish he has suffered at the hands of his daughters.

The news of Lear's treatment had reached Cordelia, and the King of France has sent an invading force to England to help restore Lear's rights to him. In Dover, where they have landed, Cordelia finds Lear and helps to restore his sanity by loving care.

While preparing to fight the French invaders, Goneril and Regan have developed a passion for Edmund. But before they can do anything about it, the battle is fought. The French lose, and Lear and Cordelia are taken prisoners.

Edmund sends Lear and Cordelia to prison with orders for them to be secretly killed. When Albany enters, he accuses Edmund of treason for plotting with Goneril against him and the interests of the state. Edmund is given the chance to defend his honor in a duel. Edgar appears in a new disguise to take up this challenge and mortally wounds Edmund. Goneril sees the handwriting on the wall and flees from the scene. Edmund confesses all his crimes as a servent enters and announces that Goneril has poisoned Regan and killed herself. Edmund then reveals that he has ordered Lear's and Cordelia's deaths. Albany sends soldiers to prevent it, but he's too late. Lear enters carrying the dead Cordelia in his arms. As he weeps for her, surrounded by the bodies of Goneril and Regan, the survivors can only stare in respectful awe.

Albany, the victor of the battle, relinquishes rule of the country to Kent and Edgar, but the worn-out Kent doesn't accept. Edgar is left to restore order in England as the bodies of the dead are carried away.

SOURCES

There may well have been an ancient king of Britain named Lear. And he may have had daughters to whom he relinquished his kingdom and his authority

when he retired at an early age. But we can only speculate about these people because there is no historic
record of such a ruler. Lear may be only a popular
myth.

By the time Shakespeare came to write about Lear,
there were several available versions of the story. We
know that Holinshed's *Chronicles*, Shakespeare's
source for several of his histories, contained a Lear
story. There was also another play performed at that
time called *The True Chronicle History of King Leir*. The
author is unknown, but there is a record of its performance in London in 1594, some 12 years before
Shakespeare's *King Lear* appeared. Edmund Spenser's
great epic poem *The Faerie Queen* also includes the Lear
story.

Some fine points differ in these stories, but Shakespeare's version is unique in one uncontestable
aspect: the others had happy endings. Some even had
a sequel showing how the "happily ever after" turned
out! And none had the Gloucester subplot. Shakespeare took the outline of this story from a contemporary romance, Sir Philip Sidney's *Arcadia*. He changed
names and adapted its theme of filial ingratitude as a
parallel to reinforce the tension and impact of his main
plot.

Since he was concerned with tragedy, not history,
Shakespeare was free to take whatever liberties he
chose in order to shape the drama to his purpose.
And that was his story of *King Lear*.

The Characters

King Lear

The title character of this play is unquestionably its
dominant figure. Although the name "Lear" comes
from some ruler who may never have actually lived,
Shakespeare has created a flesh-and-blood monarch
whose actions and reactions determine the main
course of events in the play.

You must remember that Lear is first of all a king.
He is now in his 80s and is accustomed to all the power, the authority, the responsibilities, and the privi-
leges of an absolute monarch. In our age, when such
total rule is rare, we might not really comprehend
what that means. But if you think back to every story
of every king you've ever heard about, even fairy-tale
monarchs, you'll have some idea of how the Elizabethans felt about a king.

As a man, Lear is the ruler of a family. To the Elizabethans, the family unit was just a miniature version
of the government. So the power and authority of the
father was given the same respect.

In a world where the life expectancy was much lower than our own, 80 was an exceptional age to attain.
When *King Lear* was first performed, Queen Elizabeth I
had only recently died at age 70. So as a "geriatric,"
not much would have been expected of Lear. Still,
retirement was unknown. The tradition of the day
was that you worked as long as you were able.

From the moment Lear announces his retirement,
we have to keep an eye on him to detect any sign of
weakness or infirmity, to see if the action is justified.
The physical strength it took to survive the fierce
storm would appear to contradict such a view. Even
his final act of carrying in the body of Cordelia is quite
an achievement for an 80-year-old.

But what about his mind—the moodiness, the rash judgments, the rage? Are these the telltale signs of old age or senility? You have to decide for yourself when Lear is in his right mind, when he is being manipulative, and when he is actually mad.

Lear is never entirely alone on the stage; he is attended by someone even in his most contemplative moments. But Shakespeare has given him such an aura that the spotlight is always on him and he is always in focus. We can examine his every word and every move microscopically.

Observe the skill with which he tries to manipulate his daughters. Notice how he rouses our sympathy with references to himself as "tired," "poor," and "old." You'll notice that Lear really only *acts* in the first scene and that all the rest is *reaction*. But it is the most skillful reaction imaginable since it never fails to hold our interest and attention.

In the final analysis, Lear himself must be judged on several counts. He undoubtedly triggered the forces that brought England to the brink of civil war. It took a foreign invasion to restore authority and order. This makes Lear guilty of something. But is the suffering he endures, the extent of his punishment and final loss, deserved? As you watch his progress through the play, you alone must decide whether he is indeed, " . . . a man / More sinn'd against than sinning" *(III, ii, 59–60)*.

Cordelia

The stubborn streak that Lear's youngest daughter exhibits in the first scene is the one saving gesture that redeems Cordelia from being "too good to be true."

We don't know much about Cordelia except that she is her father's favorite. As a princess, she obviously has led a privileged life, but it doesn't appear to have spoiled her as it has her older sisters.

Cordelia is not stupid. She may not be wise enough to avoid losing her share of Lear's kingdom, but she can speak up when her honor as well as interest are at stake. She makes sure that the King of France does not get the wrong idea about her error of judgment and consider it a crime.

Although she disappears from the stage after the first scene and doesn't return until the last scene of the fourth act, her image is kept before us and periodically polished. This leads to great expectations. Still, we're not disappointed when she does return to the stage. From that point on she is the soul of gentleness and goodness in her devotion to her aged father and his welfare.

By endowing Cordelia with such powerful virtue, Shakespeare seems to be indulging us in our eternal wish for the ultimate fairy-tale princess. We want her to make everything come out all right. Because it doesn't, despite her noble efforts, her last moments on the stage are all the more poignant.

Goneril

In terms of pure evil, it may be difficult to distinguish Lear's two older daughters from each other. But these are not identical twins. Goneril, whom we get to know first, is the firstborn and has an imperious manner not unlike Lear's. Highly intelligent, she has long been aware of her father's moodiness, and she decides to play it for all it's worth. Although she conspires initially with her sister Regan to protect their mutual interests, greed gets the better of her. When it combines with lust, there's no stopping this powerful force. When she is confronted with evidence of her treachery by her husband, she sneers, "Who can arraign me for't?" *(V, iii, 160.)*

As one of the three principal villains in *King Lear*, Goneril does her share to provide a broad picture of evil. And if you think she is cruel only in her behavior to her father, read her conversations with her husband and her recommendation for Gloucester's punishment. Finally, of course, who else would stoop to poison as a means of getting what she wants?

In her fancy clothes, Goneril couldn't care less about degrading her father with haggling over the size of his retinue. She is interested only in "looking after number one." And when there is no longer a way out, when she is utterly trapped in the web she has spun, only she will have the final say.

Regan

The cruelty and the evil inherent in Regan are harder to detect at first. We may be taken in as much as Lear is by her sugary words. This second daughter is extremely well spoken. She uses words as a tool and a weapon more craftily than her older sister.

As the middle child, Regan is less accustomed to initiating; she usually follows her older sister's lead, particularly if it serves her self-interest. When Lear turns to her after he has been turned out by Goneril, we can see why Regan doesn't rush to welcome him. But the force in her rejection of his request, her denial of any comfort, and her instant willingness to turn this old man out into the violent storm remind us that there is evil just below her sweet exterior.

Regan is more the stiletto to Goneril's sword. Even though Regan schemes, she is faithful in her marriage. And she kills only to try to save her husband's life. But she can be vicious and strong willed. She is capable of terrifying venom when she unleashes her fury.

If her thirst for power is her primary motivation, her powerful lust is her eventual undoing. All we can do is speculate as to whether she wanted Edmund for his body or as a partner in a future struggle for rule over England. But because Regan is always "number two," she dies without knowing that her lover could never have won the battle she would have waged.

Gloucester

Gloucester is a counterpoint to Lear. There are as many parallels as there are differences between them, though they are in similar circumstances by the end of the play.

Like Lear, Gloucester is elderly. He is gullible and easily taken in by his son Edmund. But Gloucester is no weak, infirm geriatric either. He braves the storm repeatedly to bring creature comforts to his king and master. And even after being blinded, he is capable of enduring the long trek to Dover.

Unlike Lear, Gloucester is more the "average man." He speaks plainly, with little indulgence in fancy rhetoric. He doesn't really concern himself with philosophic matters until he is pushed almost to the limit of his endurance. Gloucester doesn't ask a lot of questions. He has faith in astrology much the same way he trusts Fortune.

He must have served Lear in some senior court capacity for some time, since he isn't easily disturbed by the ebb and flow of politics. But when forced to get involved, he isn't very good at it, and ultimately suffers for his lack of cunning.

This good-natured man is also not particularly perceptive about his children. From the very beginning,

when he jokes about Edmund's birth in front of his
illegitimate son, Gloucester is singularly lacking in
vision.

But Gloucester can be very brave. He is willing to
risk his life for the king and the order and stability that
Lear represents for him.

As the protagonist of the subplot, Gloucester is its
pivot. Like Goneril and Regan—Lear's daughters
who exude evil—Gloucester's son Edmund is also
evil. To what degree is Gloucester responsible for this
evil? And is his punishment in due proportion to his
"crime"? Answering these questions will give you
greater insight into the main plot's similar situation
and Lear's own final judgment. And that, of course, is
one of the great services the character of Gloucester
performs in *King Lear*. That he can arouse emotions
and stimulate our interest in his own predicament is a
testimony to the craftsmanship of the playwright who
created him.

Edmund

Edmund and Edgar are two sides of one coin. To
say that one of these sons of the Earl of Gloucester has
a particular trait is to claim the opposite of the other.
Yet Shakespeare develops each character fully.

Edmund's villainy is obvious as soon as we see him
alone on stage and listen to what he has to say. But
during our very first introduction at the start of the
play, he looks like a victim twice over. Not only is he
the product of an illicit liaison, but duty makes him
stand by while his father cracks jokes about his birth.
Is it any wonder that Edmund has turned out the way
he has?

Still, for all his carping about his illegitimacy, the
trouble he causes and his treacherous behavior seem
well   beyond   the   point   of   fair   compensation.

Edmund's glib tongue works hard to persuade us that he's doing only what he must. It reveals a keen intelligence within his warped mind. Combined with his overpowering ambition, this intelligence makes Edmund capable of seizing every opportunity that comes his way.

The passion of Lear's older daughters is something this young adventurer barely acknowledges. He allows Fate to decide which one shall have him. Is this a more mature Edmund giving a nod to higher powers?

To observe Edmund's villainy throughout *King Lear* is to see more than a case study in evil. It also reveals the twisted path of a tortured soul.

Edgar

We probably see more facets of Gloucester's older son than of any other character in *King Lear*. He ranges from the insipid dupe we meet at the beginning of Act I, Scene ii, to the heroic heir to the kingdom in the final scene. In between we discover a lot about Edgar, primarily through his own speech and action. Very little is said to him except the slanderous comments of the bastard, Edmund. Considering the source, they are almost endearing.

Throughout the play we see an Edgar who has faith in the gods and their justice. Still, when troubles arise, he can think and act for himself. As the madman beggar, an imaginative notion to begin with, he acts the part well enough to deceive his father and godfather. And, while running wildly about in his fake madness, he manages to comfort Lear and provide extraordinary assistance for Gloucester.

We may ridicule Edgar's stupidity for allowing Edmund to drive him from his home, but we have to admire his achievement of stature at the end. There are difficult journeys for many characters in *King Lear*, and Edgar's is not an easy one. But it is ultimately and deservedly rewarding.

Albany

Another significant contrast in the play is Albany. He is almost as unlike his brother-in-law, Cornwall, as Gloucester's two sons are different.

It is easy to see why the alliance between the two poles of Albany and Cornwall would never last. Not only are their names opposites—Albany was the ancient name for Scotland, and Cornwall is located in the southwesternmost part of England—so are their temperaments. The hot and fiery Cornwall could never be compatible with the cool, calm Albany.

The foul-mouthed Goneril calls her husband Albany cowardly, but he doesn't display any lack of courage. He's enough of a military commander to win a significant victory. And he's ready to meet Edmund in one-on-one combat. More than courageous, Albany is decisive when something must be done.

Altogether, Albany is an admirable character and a fitting champion for justice. The decency of his behavior makes his wife's crueller nature stand out in bold relief.

Cornwall

As befits the role of son-in-law, especially to a king, Cornwall hasn't much to say or do when we first see him. He is willing to stand by and get his fair share as Lear parcels out the kingdom.

When we first meet him on his own turf, as a guest but nevertheless as Gloucester's "arch and patron," he is assertive and authoritative. In a matter of moments he has taken things over and is making all the important decisions.

Cornwall is evil, but certainly not a coward. It takes him a while, but he does own up to Lear that he had Kent put into the stocks. And he's ready to defend that action.

In his own mind, Cornwall is a fair judge. Having decided from Edmund's report that Gloucester is a traitor, he makes a pass at giving the old man a chance to speak for himself. But getting nowhere and not discovering anything new, Cornwall doesn't hesitate to execute the sentence with zest.

For all the violence, tempest, rage, anger, and horror in the play, only one pair of hands in *King Lear* is really bloodied. That they are Cornwall's is a mark and measure of his villainy. He is, after all, a fitting partner for the cruel Regan.

Kent

Kent is the ideal first mate to the commander of the ship of state. From the moment we meet him and observe his tactful response to Gloucester's bawdy chatter, we know we can rely on this good man. It doesn't take long for us to become better acquainted.

When Lear banishes Cordelia, and Kent speaks up in her behalf, he is bold but courteous. And he sticks to his guns, even at the risk of his own banishment.

The measure of his devotion to his master, the king, is shown by his assumption of a disguise. This enables him to continue in Lear's service.

There are several additional facets of Kent's personality. He can be hotheaded, as in the outburst that infuriates Lear in the very first scene. And his treatment of Oswald is hardly gentle. Kent even shows a sense of humor in his lengthy description of Goneril's steward.

Kent is not a great philosopher, but he does acknowledge that there are greater forces determining our fates. He endures disfavor and discomfort stoically.

His devotion and faithfulness are always in our minds. In the midst of the final turmoil, we still have compassion for Kent when he tells us that he cannot fulfill the only formal request made of him. He cannot share the responsibility for restoring order to England because he is nearing his own end. Who would deny him his final rest and reward?

The Fool

Although he is an oddity to us, the Fool was greeted by an Elizabethan audience with great familiarity. The monarch in Shakespeare's time may not have had an official court jester, but the position was a historic one. In conventional drama of the day, as a holdover from morality plays of earlier days and the traveling stock companies that wandered the countryside, the role was classic. A Fool had established characteristics and responsibilities.

Among them, the Fool had license to roam the stage and approach the audience familiarly, often joking with them and talking directly to them. He acted as a bridge between the action on stage and the audience's own experience. We might think of this today as "low comedy," but it was welcome in its day. The better the Fool, the greater his popularity with the "groundlings"—those members of the audience who stood directly around the stage (today's closest equivalent would be the fans seated in the bleachers of the ballpark).

Shakespeare exploits this aspect of the Fool to make him a character in the play as well as a commentator on the action, much the way the chorus functioned in Greek tragedy.

The notion of the Fool providing comic relief is difficult to see in the darkness of *King Lear*, but such relief does occur. This is not the thigh-slapping humor we might expect, but is more colorful relief in the very presence of the Fool as well as his bits of light verse, songs, riddles, etc. The role demands an actor physically nimble, adept at tongue-twisting speech, quick at comebacks, and intelligent enough to let the Fool's performance speak for itself.

Tradition has it that the Fool in Elizabethan tragedy is the instructor of the wise man. Speaking in riddles, the Fool repeatedly reminds Lear of his folly, which we know to be the truth. As such, the Fool is our champion, giving vent to our thoughts and emotions. No wonder audiences can't help loving the Fool. It is probably just as well that we don't see the Fool give up the ghost. Though it can be dramatically justified, we still miss the Fool during the latter half of the play.

Oswald

The role of Goneril's steward is another holdover from earlier forms of drama. Shakespeare has, however, adapted this stock character to his own purpose in *King Lear*.

Oswald is not completely the traditional two-dimensional buffoon and cowardly servant. He is brave enough, or firm enough, to resist Regan's attempt to pry information from him. Is this loyalty to Goneril? Or is it the blind following of instructions? Even when he is slain, he is true to his mission, asking his executioner to forward the messages he carries.

But Oswald is all too ready to conspire with Goneril and share her villainy. He is delighted to carry out her order to snub Lear and his retinue. In fact, it was his complaint that started the trouble between Goneril and Lear.

Of course, Oswald is really nothing compared to the arch villains of this play. Edgar has the ultimate say after he has disposed of his father's would-be killer:

> I know thee well: a serviceable villain;
> As duteous to the vices of thy mistress
> As badness would desire.
>> *(Act IV, Scene vi, lines 248–50)*

That sums up Oswald.

Other Elements

SETTING

King Lear takes place in mythological, prehistoric England. It begins in Lear's palace but never returns to that spot. Once the action starts to move, it doesn't stop until the last note of the recessional is sounded.

Geography isn't really important, although it does figure in the play. We know we are somewhere to the north at Albany's castle when Lear first quarrels with Goneril. Later we move to Gloucester's castle, within and outside the walls.

We can't miss knowing when we are outside in a storm, and it's obvious when we move inside to some form of shelter. The lack of changeable scenery made it necessary to be nonspecific, but the Elizabethan platform stage with its recess in the rear allowed for certain suggestions of movement and place.

Eventually, the action moves to the southeast of England. Edgar guides the blind Gloucester toward Dover, where the king's party has already been sent. Eventually the two meet.

The French have obviously landed in that area, and Cordelia catches up with Lear and has him brought to her camp to rest. It is not far from there that the final battle is fought and the action of the play is resolved.

The rapid flow of events in *King Lear* makes what is happening infinitely more interesting than where it takes place.

THEMES

There is a wide range of themes running through *King Lear*. Often they are straightforward, but just as frequently they are buried or seemingly contradictory.

It's important to remember that Shakespeare makes many points by parallel or contrasting words and actions. If something is significant in the main plot, it will probably turn up in some fashion in the subplot, and vice versa.

Some of the important themes are:

The Folly of Old Age—The Ingratitude of Youth

Lear's division of his kingdom, his "early retirement," unleashes the forces that lead ultimately to the catastrophic ending of the play. Gloucester is no less responsible for his calamity, for being rash in his judgment of his older son and blindly trusting his younger. Are these men senile? How much of the suffering that they endure do they deserve?

And considering how they are abused by their fathers, don't Edgar and Goneril deserve some sympathy, some satisfaction? Regan, too—should she have to put up with her father's rowdy entourage? Or are these, indeed, thankless children? Do they try to grab more than is rightfully theirs?

There are several references to how "golden-agers" should be looked after by their children. What do you think of those making the comments, as well as those they're discussing? How you feel, how your sympathies shift, will affect your attitude toward the ending of *King Lear*.

Good and Evil

With the exception of momentary lapses, the good characters in this play are all very good, and the bad characters are quite evil. Other than the heads of the two families, Lear and Gloucester, there is little growth or development. But those characters undergo such profound experiences that there is enough internal activity to keep the play moving forward.

Other characters talk about benign or malevolent forces, but Lear wrestles with them head-on. His plunge into insanity is marked by his ever-increasing awareness of the presence of good and evil in areas he had never before considered. And even the generally placid Gloucester exhibits new awareness as he proceeds toward his final moment.

Since the play ends with the death of all those we have come to love, except those who must carry on, it has been called a study in pessimism. Do you accept that judgment? Or do you see redeeming aspects? Is the play only about a struggle between good and evil or is there a broader interpretation?

Nature

Shakespeare's concept of nature in *King Lear* is a kaleidoscopic picture of the prevailing Elizabethan attitude. It is not always the picture we expect, but all the pieces are there.

The Elizabethans viewed nature as order. It consisted of a universe in which there was an established hierarchy; everything had its own relative position. Heaven, the Divine Being, and the stars and planets were all above. On earth, the king was at the head of the class structure, with the nobles next, and on down to the peasantry, and beneath them were the lowliest humans: beggars, lunatics, and so on. Below that came the animals.

When this order was disturbed, things were considered unnatural or "monstrous." Chaos ruled the unnatural, and malevolent forces were involved.

There are constant references to nature and unnatural things and forces throughout the play. Shakespeare was deeply concerned with this concept and stretched it to the limit in *King Lear*. Did he finally believe that such a system existed and operated in the determination of man's fate? Your interpretation of the play should provide you with the answer to this question.

Vision and Blindness

There are more overt references to vision and blindness than almost any other theme. There are subtle variations woven through the drama, too. Obviously, when someone is behaving intelligently, he has vision. Conversely, he acts blindly when he does something foolish.

You may notice what seem to be contradictions. For example, madness is folly and should produce blindness. But in the midst of Lear's madness, he comes up with some provocative insights. What does this tell us?

Don't come to a hasty conclusion about the theme of vision and blindness. Evaluate the obvious references in the text, and consider the theme as it applies to the characters' actions throughout the play.

STYLE

A new student of Shakespeare will find *King Lear* quite different from any contemporary play. Elizabethan drama had its own set of rules, and Shakespeare was guided, if not bound, by most of them.

Most noticeable is the somewhat formal speech in verse. You may have heard about Shakespeare's iambic pentameter, which is nothing more than a description of a poetic form—a five-beat line with a stress on every second syllable. It's used frequently, though not exclusively, in *King Lear*. This was simply Shakespeare's way of approximating the sound of upper-class speech or the way it was believed serious matters should sound when discussed. In addition, there is his use of verse. Poetry gave him the opportunity to say a lot in a few words.

Don't read the dialogue in a singsong pattern. Just read it straight through and let the punctuation guide you to the rests and stopping points. After a while it will become as natural as reading prose.

Shakespeare breaks the monotony of the verse with prose speech when appropriate. How certain forms are used at certain times can be very revealing.

ELIZABETHAN ENGLISH

All languages change. Differences in pronunciation and word choice are apparent even between parents and their children. If language differences can appear in one generation, it is only to be expected that the English used by Shakespeare four hundred years ago will diverge markedly from the English that is used today. The following information on Shakespeare's language will help a modern reader to a fuller understanding of *King Lear*.

Mobility of Word Classes

Adjectives, nouns, and verbs were less rigidly confined to particular classes in Shakespeare's day. Nouns were often used as verbs. In Act I, Scene i, the King of France uses *monsters* in a context where modern usage would require "makes it appear monstrous."

> Sure her offense
> Must be of such unnatural degree
> That monsters it . . . .
> *(lines 217-19)*

Adjectives could be used as adverbs. In Act I, Scene iv, line 230 Lear says: "I should be false persuaded" whereas the modern equivalent would require *falsely*. They could also be used as verbs, as in Act II, Scene ii, line 118, where *worthy* becomes a verb meaning "win honor for" in: "That worthied him."

Changes in Word Meaning

The meanings of words undergo changes, a process that can be illustrated by the fact that *chip* extended its meaning from a small piece of wood to a small piece of silicon. Many of the words in Shakespeare still exist today but their meanings have changed. The change may be small, as in the case of *comfortable*, which meant "comforting, ready to give comfort," as in: "I have another daughter, / Who, I am sure, is kind and comfortable." (I,iv,304-5) Or the change in meaning is more fundamental, as when *character* meant "handwriting" (I,i,260), *curious* meant "elaborate" (I,iii,32), *fond* meant "foolish" (I,iv,299), *presently* meant "immediately" (I,ii,98), *prevented* meant "came before, forestalled" (I,i,44), and *teem* meant "have children": "If she must teem, / Create her child of spleen . . . ." (I,iv,279-80).

Vocabulary Loss

Words not only change their meanings, but are frequently discarded from the language. In the past, *leman* meant "sweetheart" and *sooth* meant "truth." The following words used in *King Lear* are no longer current in English, but their meanings can usually be gauged from the contexts in which they occur:

brazed *(I, i, 10)*: hardened
knave *(I, i, 20)*: fellow
champains *(I, i, 68)*: grassy plains

sectary astronomical *(I, ii, 147):* student of, believer in astrology

clotpoll *(I, iv, 46):* blockhead

epicurism *(I, iv, 241):* gluttony

kibes *(I, v, 9):* chilblains

gasted *(II, i, 54):* frightened

bewray *(II, i, 106):* discover, reveal

finical *(II, ii, 17):* fastidiousness

cullionly *(II, ii, 31):* rascally

front *(II, ii, 105):* forehead

meiny *(II, iv, 34):* servants

fetches *(II, iv, 86):* tricks

bemadding *(III, i, 38):* maddening

caitiff *(III, ii, 55):* wretch

out-paramoured *(III, iv, 89):* had more mistresses than

corky *(III, vii, 29):* withered

sot *(IV, ii, 8):* fool

simples *(IV, iv, 14):* medicinal herbs

whelked *(IV, vi, 71):* twisted

fitchew *(IV, vi, 121):* polecat, prostitute

list *(V, iii, 62):* wish

Verbs

Shakespearean verb forms differed from modern usage in three main ways:

1. Questions and negatives could be formed without using *do/did* as when Edmund asks:

> Why brand they us
> With base?

> *(I, ii, 9–10)*

whereas today we would say: "Why do they brand us as base, low born?" Another example occurs when Gloucester states: "I know not"; modern usage demands: "I do not know." Review the lists that follow. Shakespeare had the option of forms a and b, whereas contemporary usage permits only form a.

a	b
How do you look?	How look you?
How did he look?	How looked he?
You do not look well.	You look not well.
You did not look well.	You looked not well.

2. A number of past participles and past tense verb forms are used that would be ungrammatical today. Among these are *strucken* for "struck": "I'll not be strucken, my Lord" *(I, iv, 83); writ* for "written": ". . . I have writ my sister" *(I, iv, 338); forbid* for "forbidden": "This courtesy forbid thee shall the Duke / Instantly know. . . ." *(III, iii, 21); holp* for "helped": ". . . he holp the heavens to rain." *(III, vii, 60);* and *spoke* for "spoken": "Ere you had spoke so far." *(V, iii, 64).*

3. Archaic verb forms sometimes occur with *thou* and *he/she/it*.

> Follow me; thou shalt serve me.
>
> *(I, iv, 40)*

> Thou wast a pretty fellow when thou hadst no
>   need to care . . .
>
> *(I, iv, 188)*

> What he hath uttered. . . .
>
> *(I, iv, 330)*

Pronouns

Shakespeare and his contemporaries had one extra pronoun, *thou*, which could be used in addressing a person who was one's equal or social inferior. *You* was obligatory if more than one person was addressed: "Tell me, my daughters / . . . Which of you . . ." *(I, i, 47ff).* But *you* could also be used to indicate respect, as when Goneril told her father: "Sir, I love you more than words can wield the matter . . ." *(I, i, 54).*

Frequently, a person in power used *thou* to a subordinate but was addressed *you* in return, as when Edmund and Curan speak.

> *Edmund:* Save thee, Curan.
>   *Curan:* And you, sir. I have been with your
>   father.
>
> (II, i, 1ff)

But if *thou* was used inappropriately, it might be offensive. The Fool uses *thou* when speaking to Lear to underline the fact that Lear has given away his power along with his lands.

> O nuncle, court holy water in a dry house is better than this rain-water out o'door. Good nuncle, in; ask thy daughters' blessing: here's a night pities neither wise men nor fools.
>
> (III, ii, 10ff)

One further pronominal reference warrants a comment. Lear uses the royal plural *we* when he has or thinks he has power.

> Right noble Burgundy,
> When she was dear to us, we did hold her so;
> (I, i, 194ff)

But he changes to *I* as he begins to appreciate his weakness:

> Howl, howl, howl, howl!—O, you are men of
>   stones:
> Had I your tongues and eyes, I'd use them so
> That heaven's vault should crack.
>
> (V, iii, 256ff)

Prepositions

Prepositions were less standardized in Elizabethan English than they are today, and so we find several uses in *King Lear* that would have to be modified in contemporary speech. Among these are *on* for "by," as in: ". . . as if we were villains on necessity . . ." *(I, ii, 118); with* for "by" in: "He is attended with a desperate train . . ." *(II, iv, 303); of* for "by" in: "Unwhipped of justice . . ." *(III, ii, 53);* and *in* for "into" in:

> There is a cliff whose high and bending head
> Looks fearfully in the confinèd deep . . .
>
> *(IV, i, 73)*

Multiple Negation

Contemporary English requires only one negative per statement and regards such utterances as "I haven't none" as nonstandard. Shakespeare often used two or more negatives for emphasis:

> *Gloucester:* He cannot be such a monster.
> *Edmund:* Nor is not, sure.
>
> *(I, ii, 91ff)*

And Lear says: "No eyes in your head, nor no money in your purse?" *(IV, vi, 142ff)*

FORM AND STRUCTURE

Elizabethan plays were written to be performed in circumstances peculiar to their time. A wooden platform thrust out into the audience could serve as a stage. Although even the poorest performing troupe indulged in the most elaborate costumes they could afford, there was no scenery and no special lighting.

A private performance might be held indoors, but most were outside. Theaters of the time were modeled after inn courtyards with tiered galleries running around the perimeter. The cheapest admission was for the ground area where there were no seats, so the audience stood or roamed about.

Actors—there were no actresses; men performed all the roles—entered from the back of the stage area left and right, and exited the same way. Sometimes there was a recessed area in the back across which a curtain might be drawn when appropriate.

There was no signal—no curtain coming down, no lowering of the lights—to indicate a change of scene or act. Action at a particular place ended when all the characters involved left the stage. The best available records or scripts of Shakespeare's plays therefore don't contain the act and scene divisions we commonly use today. *King Lear* was written to be performed under these circumstances. These conditions dictated its form and structure, which should actually be viewed as one uninterrupted piece.

One way Shakespeare maintains pace and interest is to alternate scenes between the main plot and the subplot. As the story line unfolds, he interweaves other scenes—Albany's castle, Cordelia's tent—but the focus shifts back and forth between Lear's story and Gloucester's.

Shakespeare also balances these changing scenes with a range of dynamics. The howling intensity of the storm scenes, for example, is interrupted before the high pitch loses its effect. Each time we return to Lear and the thunder and lightning, we expect a little more; we are wound up and ready rather than exhausted by the tumult.

The parallel and contrasting aspects of the two plots also create an undercurrent of interest. They combine to give the play stimulus as well as dramatic texture.

Within the limitations of what we consider "primitive" theatrical technology, Shakespeare applied his special skills in *King Lear* to produce an experience of profound theatrical tragedy, a riveting drama.

The Story
ACT I
ACT I, SCENE I

Just mention the words *King Lear* and an image springs to mind—the famous division of the kingdom among his daughters. It's one of the most memorable scenes in all of Shakespeare's works. It's also one of the longest opening scenes, loaded with important details that set up all the following events.

The play begins in a sort of "no-man's-land," but it soon becomes King Lear's court, when he enters and quickly establishes himself as the reigning monarch.

This opening scene introduces all the major characters of the main plot and even gives a quick preview of the subplot. There is nothing wishy-washy about these characters. What they say and what they do reveal a great deal about them, at least enough to start your impressions building.

NOTE: On stage, the characters seem to fall into vivid groupings. Throughout the play there will be many times when sides are drawn; it will be interesting to see which side has the greater weight.

Lines 1–6

The play begins with a casual conversation between two members of the court, the Earl of Kent and the Earl of Gloucester. They observe that the king has treated his two sons-in-law, Albany and Cornwall, inconsistently. Remember, nothing said by any character is ever a "throwaway." Even these first few lines have some bearing on what will occur later. Right at the start, they begin to paint a picture of an unpredictable monarch.

Lines 7–33

With no more said about that, they turn to a third character—Edmund, the Earl of Gloucester's bastard son. Listen to the way his father speaks about his origin, right in front of him. Put yourself in Edmund's position and think how you would feel if your father spoke that way about your less-than-respectable birth.

Gloucester is good-natured, but oblivious to a son's feelings. Look at the rude contrast he makes when he says:

> . . . there was good sport at his making, and the whoreson must be acknowledged. Do you know this noble gentleman, Edmund?
>
> *(lines 21–24)*

NOTE: The actor playing Edmund wouldn't have to make a spoken comment about his feelings on this subject. He would have to have a physical response that the audience could see. This early in the play, a brief moment like this should serve notice for us to watch carefully for reactions. Sometimes it will be easy to tell, such as a spoken "aside." Sometimes it will be silence. Sometimes it will be a violent physical response. They offer clues to what is happening inside the character's mind.

This introductory dialogue ends with Edmund, the "whoreson," and Kent, the "noble gentleman," making polite acquaintance. The sound of an offstage trumpet suddenly announces the arrival of the royal party.

Lines 34–120

The whole tone of the play now changes. We have been listening to characters speak in prose, loose and informal. Now verse takes over as the king enters in all his majesty, followed in precise order of rank by his court.

NOTE: The Natural Order   This strict placement—the positioning of king at the head, dukes and duchesses next, earls, then other nobles, and so on down the line—was important in Elizabethan England. This was the way things were supposed to be. It confirmed that all was well. It was "natural," the way nature intended things to be. An upset of this would be considered "monstrous," and we will soon see what happens when that occurs.

The first breach comes when Lear announces that he intends to retire and will divide his kingdom equally among his three daughters—Goneril, Regan, and Cordelia. Making this announcement, he's firm and authoritative. Nothing suggests weakness or senility. Only his white hair reminds us that he is, after all, an aged man and king.

Before allotting their particular territories, Lear asks each daughter to make a profession of her love and devotion to him. Then he will decide who gets a larger and more advantageous share. Talk about sibling rivalry!

Is this capricious? Or has everything been already decided? Is Lear telling just a little fib? Maybe, but Shakespearean "fibs" have a way of growing and taking on a much bigger importance.

Besides playing with his daughters' affections, he's indulging himself, too, by putting on a show of his power. It's all a game, he seems to say.

Goneril and Regan know the rules. They can tell fibs, too. Their polished speeches certainly don't sound very sincere. How much truth is there in their vast professions of love and devotion? As they lay it on, one thicker than the next, Lear's youngest daughter, Cordelia, warns us in asides that there is trouble ahead.

Lines 69–76

Now it's Cordelia's turn, and the warning bears fruit. What can she say to gain a larger share than her sisters?

> *Lear:*   Speak
> Cor: Nothing, my lord.
> *Lear:* Nothing?
> Cor: Nothing.
> *Lear:* Nothing will come of nothing. Speak
>   again.
>
> *(lines 87–91)*

Lear has been judging his daughters on quantity, not quality. His whole idea of value appears to be bound up in this idea of "How much do you love me?" Cordelia's blunt inability to offer something, anything, is an affront to him. Father and daughter speak in short, staccato dialogue, underscoring the tense emotion of the confrontation.

But what really is Cordelia's problem? She could be completely honest when she says that she simply speaks the truth and performs her duty. Some might feel this is a stubborn streak coming out. Others might feel she's being a little feisty. Maybe she's gambling, taking a chance that her perverse honesty will trick Lear into giving her a larger portion. We haven't seen enough of Cordelia to form an impression of absolute goodness personified.

Lear, meanwhile, is not at all satisfied with her answer. A dramatic moment is building. Lear stalls. Has he really heard such an "unnatural" reply?

> *Lear:* So young, and so untender?
> Cor: So young, my lord, and true.
>
> *(lines 107–8)*

A standoff. Neither side will compromise. It is all or *nothing*. That is unacceptable to Lear. Listen to his pronouncement of judgment. Rage and violence seem to pour forth way out of proportion as he exercises his absolute rights as a father and a king.

He calls on the gods above to witness his withdrawal of Cordelia's share. And then he goes further: he disowns her, he banishes her from his sight.

NOTE: The scales of justice have now tipped. This is our first demonstration of judgment, of crime and punishment. It will recur in many different forms as the play unfolds.

There's still a chance for reconsideration, but time is running on. And both sides are stubborn.

Lines 121–187

To provide a case for the defendant, Kent, the loyal attendant, steps forward. Drawing on his long and faithful service to Lear, he speaks thoughts that may well run through the audience's mind. He begs Lear to retract the sentence.

No, the king has spoken. Authority must be preserved even though he is giving it away in almost the next breath.

> Only we shall retain
> The name, and all th' addition to a king. The
>   sway,
> Revènue, execution of the rest,
> Belovèd sons, be yours; which to confirm,
> This coronet part between you.
>
> *(lines 135–39)*

For himself, Lear will keep a retinue of one hundred knights who will accompany him on monthly visits to Goneril and Regan in turn. But all the rest he thrusts away with the parting gesture of the coronet, the symbol of rule.

NOTE: If there is any question of an inversion of the natural order, that settles it. He would no longer be king, on top, nor father, on top. It must lead to problems of real magnitude. It must lead to some form of "chaos."

Meanwhile, Kent persists. Again citing his past service as his support, he makes the first reference to Lear's *madness* in executing such a rash judgment. Moreover, he questions Lear's vision, the ability to see his own folly. But Lear rejects his plea.

> Out of my sight!
>
> *(line 157)*

In a last-ditch effort, Kent begs:

> See better, Lear, and let me still remain
> The true blank of thine eye.
>
> *(lines 158–59)*

Lear will have none of this. Again, judgment and sentence are swift: Kent, too, is banished. The king is still in command.

In his parting words, Kent asks the gods to provide shelter for Cordelia, who has been, from his viewpoint, just in her behavior.

Lines 188–266

Gloucester, who left the stage with Edmund right after the royal party arrived, now brings in Cordelia's suitors, the Duke of Burgundy and the King of France. When he is offered Cordelia's hand without a dowry, Burgundy rejects it flatly. He's not interested in the maid without the money, so to speak.

Did Cordelia suspect this? Is this why she deliberately alienated Lear, so that she wouldn't be forced to marry the blunt Burgundy?

When the King of France is given the same offer, he questions the sudden change in Lear's affections. What could be the reason?

> Sure her offense
> Must be of such unnatural degree
> That monsters it . . .
>
> *(lines 217–19)*

Is Cordelia afraid that he will believe her guilty of some violent crime, and that she will lose him? Is there a suggestion of preference when she interjects a plea that Lear confirm her only sin to be a lack of "that glib and oily art / To speak and purpose not . . . ." *(lines 224–25)*? She reminds Lear and all those on stage, as well as in the audience, that her disfavor stems from no criminal act.

France is not easily dissuaded. He sees the paradox of Cordelia's "richness" shining through her newly poverished situation. He loves her for her virtues, not her dowry. He accepts her despite her banishment.

What a contrast to Lear's quick judgment. Which of the two kings on stage, which of the two sides, do you think now has the audience's sympathy?

With nothing further to say, with no further consideration, no further reason applied, Lear turns his eyes away from his former favorite child and leaves the stage, followed in procession by his entourage.

Lines 267–283

Goneril and Regan have lingered behind. With her new protector at her side, Cordelia bids farewell to them. She states clearly that she knows what they are really like, but asks them to transcend their faults and take care of their father after she has gone. In terse replies that could have come straight out of any version of Cinderella, they tell her to mind her own business, to take care of her own prince, who has accepted her despite her poor *fortune*.

NOTE: The image of fortune—sometimes Fortune, and sometimes fortune's wheel—will appear throughout the play. To the Elizabethan audience it always suggested change: what is on top now will inevitably fall to the bottom later—and vice versa. Fortune and her wheel are never static.

Lines 284–306

After Cordelia and France have left, the tone changes again. Verse, poetry, and rhetoric are left behind as the two sisters speak plainly to one another. Looking back at Lear's rash and hasty behavior, they're obviously concerned. Who wouldn't be? They attribute his banishment of Cordelia and Kent to the weakness of old age, which they claim is not new in him. There's strength in unity, and they agree to consult and take joint action when the situation warrants.

As the stage clears, you have to start making up your own mind about these outspoken characters. Is Lear the intolerable tyrant he appears to be? Is Cordelia as sweet and good as she seems? And what of the two older sisters? What have they done but confirm a parent's image of his own goodness? Everyone has heard a mother or father, if not their own, ask a child, "How much do you love me?" But at Lear's obvious age, and in his position, the question comes a little late. And dangerously.

ACT I, SCENE II

NOTE: No curtain fell, no lights were lowered, but the Elizabethan audience knew the scene had changed when the stage cleared and a character or group entered. Perhaps a slight change of costume or a portable prop would help define the new place or circumstances.

Lines 1–22

Since Edmund had left the stage early in the previous scene, he had an opportunity to make some slight change in his attire to suggest that he was now "at home" in Gloucester's castle as he enters the stage alone.

Within moments he has revealed that he was not a dispassionate bystander to his father's naive insults. He calls on nature, whom he swears to serve. But what nature does he mean? Certainly not the nature of law and order. No, for Edmund, who is himself *unnatural* by birth, his nature is the law of might, of wit and cunning—the law of the jungle.

His illegitimacy is indeed a sore point as is his status as younger son. But why should he be subject to that order which would deprive him of his inheritance? Why should his brother, by the mere accident of his preceding birth, get it all? By design, Edmund wishes to overturn the other, the truly natural order, and through his cleverness take all. He cheerfully and boldly calls on his gods to witness his resolution and support him in his endeavors.

Lines 23–114

Gloucester walks in and Edmund immediately resumes the pose of the sweet and modest young man we saw in the first scene. Pretending rather obviously to hide a letter in his hand, he stimulates his father's curiosity. When asked what he is reading, Edmund replies: "Nothing, my lord" *(line 31)*.

Where have we heard that before? But when another parent received that same reply, it stayed there, rooted to its "nothingness." Here, it leads to "something." This father, at least, tries to demonstrate that he has some vision.

> Let's see. Come, if it be nothing, I shall not need spectacles.
>
> *(lines 34–35)*

> Let's see, let's see!
>
> *(line 42)*

NOTE: The recurring theme of vision and blindness grows heavier and heavier at this early stage. Remember, the Elizabethans considered the eyes the entrance to the mind, the intelligence and reason. If a person had vision, he could behave reasonably. Without it, passion ruled and folly usually followed.

But while Gloucester's intentions are proper and true, the object is false. Edmund hands him a forged letter from his brother Edgar, which starts out with a condemnation of the accepted order, the tradition that makes a young man wait for the death of an old parent to come into his inheritance. It goes on to scorn this policy and suggests that the two brothers take action to rectify the situation and thus share their father's property while they are young.

Gloucester, good-natured, affable soul that he is, questions the letter's authenticity. Again and again he asks questions, delaying a response as long as possible. When Edmund "reluctantly" swears that the handwriting is Edgar's, that he has even heard his brother make some suggestions that sons should

replace fathers at a certain age, only then does
Gloucester cry out that Edgar is a villain.

How easily is Gloucester gulled? The simple ruse of
a forged letter is not much by intellectual standards,
but dramatically it was a pretty well-established con-
vention and the audience would not have been too
harsh on him. Still, it represents a turning point in this
subplot parallel to the main plot.

But rather than attribute it immediately to pure villainy on his son's part, Gloucester recalls that there
have been outside influences at work. The signs have
been the strange aberrations of "nature," which are
omens of what has now happened.

> This villain of mine comes under the prediction,
> there's son against father; the King falls from bias
> of nature; there's father against child.
>
> *(lines 107–9)*

Gloucester does not pronounce sentence. He reserves
final judgment as Edmund is ordered to provide further evidence.

Lines 115–29

Alone again, Edmund sneers at the old man's references to the celestial origins of earthly problems. So
much for astrology. But can you dismiss it so easily?
After all, look who is turning up his nose at the influence of "other powers."

Nevertheless, under any circumstances, Edmund
makes the claim that will echo throughout literature
and the performing arts for ages: I am what I am.

Lines 130–77

Edmund is in a lighthearted mood as Edgar enters,
setting the plot against the unsuspecting older brother
into motion. He sighs "like Tom o' Bedlam" *(line 132)*
and continues to mock his absent father.

The double-dealing scoundrel soon convinces Edgar that he has aroused Gloucester's violent displeasure and has reason to fear his father's wrath. The trusting Edgar suspects nothing; he accepts Edmund's lies ever so easily. Edgar sends him to his chambers to await further news of the case against him and warns him not to go about unarmed.

With "A credulous father, and a brother noble" *(line 172)*, Edmund is riding high on Fortune's wheel. He repeats his vow to gain by wit what he cannot have by birth.

Does it seem too simple? Does the execution of Edmund's villainy happen too easily? But haven't we all been "suckered" into some practical joke through something we saw as obvious only afterward?

ACT I, SCENE III

The major characters have now all made their appearance and you've had a chance to form an opinion of each. The principal conflicts that set off the action of the main plot and the subplot have been introduced, too. It's time to enlarge upon our greater interest—the story of Lear and his daughters—and move the action forward.

Lines 1–26
The scene shifts to a new grouping on the stage, and within a matter of moments we know that we are in the Duke of Albany's castle, where his wife Goneril is speaking to her steward.

NOTE: The fawning servant was a stock character in Elizabethan drama, just as we have stock characters today—the "best friend," the butler, and so on.

The audience would expect Goneril's steward to be a groveling lackey, but Shakespeare makes special use of him.

We see him now complaining that he was struck for merely scolding the king's jester, the Fool. Goneril seizes on this to generalize on the abuse she and her household have suffered from Lear's knights and her father's rude behavior. She will retaliate by frosty behavior of her own and she encourages the steward, Oswald, to do likewise. For starters, Goneril will not be there when the king returns from hunting. Obviously, he is hale and healthy enough to enjoy that royal pastime. Goneril leaves to write to Regan, encouraging her to do likewise when Lear goes to her for his monthly visit.

People are forever making judgments in *King Lear*, usually hasty judgments at that. Goneril takes the word of a servant without hearing the other side. Is it because this suits her frame of mind? But what if the report is accurate? Can she be blamed for becoming angry at Lear's and his knights' raucous, abusive behavior? So we really don't know yet whether she is at fault for making a snap judgment that Lear's entourage is behaving badly. It's too soon to say who is the victim and who is the villain.

One slight clue is given, however. In the first scene Lear initiated the action, he set the wheels in motion. As he is spoken of in this scene, and as we shall see hereafter, he now *responds* to the actions of others. And his reactions, as we have seen, are usually passionate, to say the least.

ACT I, SCENE IV

Appearance and reality are not only thematic undertones; they actually surface purposefully in *King Lear*. We've already seen the appearance of geriatric humility and the reality of autocratic wrath, the two-faced behavior of the scoundrel Edmund, the false letter. Now we see actual disguise as Kent enters and announces that he has altered his appearance and taken on the trappings of a humble peasant in order to get close to Lear, to continue to serve his master.

Clothing obviously defines the wearer, and no aspect, from a single thread to a fully naked body, should be ignored. Is that any different from today? Don't we still judge people by what they wear?

Lines 7–40

For the second time in the play, Lear makes an entrance. This time he is in his "retirement" and is obviously enjoying it as much as any golden-ager who might have just returned from the golf course. As he meets up with Kent, he interrogates him as an executive might interview a job applicant. Kent comes up with the right answers, citing Lear's look of "authority" as the reason he wishes to serve him, and is accepted on a trial basis. No snap judgments here. Lear is a model of rational behavior if a little given to the enjoyment of flattery.

Lines 41–89

Still the spoiled autocrat, Lear claps his hands and demands his dinner and his Fool. And where is his daughter, who should be there to greet him? Oswald's brief dash across the stage provides no answers. Furthermore, a knight comes back with the information that not only is Goneril not well enough to do her duty, but he had received a curt reply from Oswald. His report of rudeness and poor treatment by the household staff prompts Lear to recall that he had observed similar behavior of late—"a most faint neglect" (line 65). Notice how mild this judgment is. Still, he is irritable because his fool is nowhere to be seen. This absence is attributed by the knight to the greater absence of another—Cordelia.

> Since my young lady's going into France, sir, the
> Fool hath much pined away.
>
> *(lines 70–71)*

Cordelia's image is kept before us through obvious references such as this, and even slighter, brief mentions. In absence, the picture of her and her goodness grows.

But first, Oswald's rudeness is dealt with. For his insolence, Lear goes to slap him and Kent trips him, earning his master's thanks and a tip as the Fool makes his entrance.

Lines 90–190

With wit, verve, and dash the Fool interrupts the mounting tension while making his own points and actually adding fuel to the fire.

Haven't you thought it pretty foolish of Lear, who is obviously physically capable of executing his duties as king, to dispose of his kingdom—his job, his authority, his possessions—so unwisely? Well, here is the Fool to put your point of view across. Were it not for his special position, he couldn't get away with the barbs he levels at Lear. In short order, he tells the monarch that he became a fool himself when he gave away his crown. Lear himself reversed the natural order when he dropped his pants and handed his daughters the rod to beat him with. In fact, to certify that he has become a fool, the lowest level of the natural order, Lear gave away his title and stripped himself symbolically naked.

Why does Lear tolerate these cutting reproaches? Why should he, the ruler, put up with the Fool, the servant? Has the reference to the Fool's beloved mistress in France triggered a sense of repentance for his

injustice in banishing her for a slight offense? Or has
the mixture of nonsense spread a cover over the cutting edge of these barbs?

Harping on the substantive, the quantitative, the
Fool asks Lear, "Can you make no use of nothing,
Nuncle?" *(lines 123–24)*, and Lear replies that "Nothing can be made out of nothing." No, Lear has not
learned that lesson.

The Fool is threatened with a whipping as Goneril
enters. But the Fool has a final word to say about
"something" and "nothing": "I am a fool," he tells
Lear, "thou art nothing" *(lines 184–185)* as he turns his
attention and his taunts to Goneril.

Lines 191–280

She accuses Lear's knights of insolence and complains that he does nothing about it when she informs
him of their abuse of her hospitality.

What is Lear's reaction? He mocks her with sar-
casm. He poses rhetorical questions. Who is this person to whom she would speak so? He plays the fool, a
fool so blind that when he asks again if anyone can tell
him who he is, the Fool replies, "Lear's shadow" *(line
221)*.

But Goneril will not put up with this. She tells him
straight out to stop his pranks. "As you are old and
reverend, should be wise" *(line 230)*. She tells him that
his knights treat her home as though it were a tavern
or a brothel.

Does Lear pay attention to what she is saying?
Hardly. Does he consider that her complaints may
have some basis in fact? Not for a minute. Instead he
uses high-flown rhetoric to shout her down, barely
noticing Albany's arrival. He curses her in no uncer-
tain terms: "Degenerate bastard," "destested kite."
The invectives pour forth from his lips with the same
fury he unleashed against Cordelia earlier.

Albany's attempts as peacemaker fail and Lear summons up his final curse. He now calls on nature, his goddess of righteous indignation, to take his part and make Goneril sterile so that she will never know the honor of a child. If she does bear, let the child turn against her so that she may know:

> How sharper than a serpent's tooth it is
> To have a thankless child.
>
> *(lines 279–80)*

The question must be asked—Does Goneril deserve such a curse, the concentrated force of such hideous wishes?

Lines 281–301

Albany is bewildered by the scene he has witnessed, but Goneril remains calm. She can handle it.

Lear returns with a mysterious reference to half his retinue, which we later discover Goneril has given orders to leave within two weeks.

His anger is almost uncontrollable, but he will contain himself. Venting his final curses on her, he vows to put out his own eyes if ever they weep as a result of Goneril's treatment. He tells her that he has another, kinder daughter, Regan, who will surely avenge him savagely when she hears what has happened. Furthermore, she will discover that he has not abandoned all the prerogatives of the monarchy.

Lines 302–39

Albany tries to insert a voice of reason, but Goneril has been too incited by Lear's curses. It's dangerous, she claims, to let him keep a hundred knights about him so that he may arm them against any imagined enemy. She summons Oswald and sends him to Regan with her side of the story, telling him to embellish it as much as he needs to produce the right effect. As for Albany, well, she can only overlook his mild manner and ignore his warnings.

Any doubts about Goneril's ability to take a firm stand are probably gone by now. Still, what has she really done? We have not seen the cause of their conflict, but have only the reports to consider, as well as their responses. The case for either side is still open.

We are beginning to have some feeling, some reaction to Albany. It should be interesting to see how the other son-in-law comes across compared to this one, who has not lined up that closely on his wife's side.

ACT I, SCENE V

Lear returns to the stage, still dressed as before, still very much the picture of a king, but without fanfare, with no royal trappings, with only Kent and the Fool at his side. He immediately sends Kent off with a letter to Regan. He, however, in striking contrast to the instructions Goneril gave to her messenger, tells Kent to stick strictly to the facts in the letter.

When Kent has departed, Lear is left alone with the Fool, who immediately tries to amuse Lear, but the turmoil is growing inside the old man. He is obviously not paying attention and his thoughts drift. When he comes out with comments such as "I did her wrong" *(line 21)*, is he thinking of Goneril or Cordelia?

Prompted by the Fool's admonition that he had grown old before he had acquired wisdom, Lear cracks a little under the strain of holding his wits together and implores heaven not to let him be mad. Already he suspects and probably knows that this would be the worst fate of all.

This brief scene probably isn't enough to turn around your attitude if you feel that he has behaved

badly up till now and really doesn't deserve much
sympathy. But as Lear's defenses begin to weaken,
you may start to react more favorably toward him
after seeing this brief display of his humanity.

ACT II

ACT II, SCENE I

If the last scene was essentially quiet and contemplative, despite the Fool's attempts at merriment, this
scene will be a marked contrast. We are back at
Gloucester's castle where Curan, a servant, is giving
Edmund the latest news.

Lines 1–19

Curan reports that Gloucester has just been
informed that Cornwall and Regan are en route and
expected that evening. He passes along the gossip
that there is already a growing unrest between the
Albany and Cornwall factions. Edmund decides on
the spot that this unexpected arrival will distract the
old Earl and presents a great opportunity to cement
his case against his brother. He calls the hidden Edgar
to the stage.

Lines 20–32

As Edgar appears, Edmund is all urgency and
warnings. The older brother is told that Gloucester
has posted guards and has them searching for him.
Moreover, is it possible that Edgar has spoken against
Cornwall, who is heading for the castle right now? Or
against Albany?

Claiming that Gloucester's arrival, which he has
just heard, signals doom for Edgar if he doesn't make
a convincing departure, Edmund prompts his brother
to engage in a fake duel with him and flee. Edgar is
convinced, does as he is told, and hurries away.

Lines 32–85

The sly Edmund then wounds himself and continues the fraud as Gloucester enters with servants carrying torches.

Edmund is really into his act now as Gloucester asks him three times where Edgar is. Stalling so that Edgar can get beyond reach and not contradict his story right away, he finally sends off the searching party. We can only guess that he pointed in the wrong direction.

He then sets about convincing Gloucester of his brother's villainy—shaping his own treacherous thoughts to fit his brother's profile—claiming he was asked to join but was opposed to Edgar's "unnatural purpose" *(line 50)*. His refusal was the cause of the duel that just took place, he says.

Gloucester needs no further proof. He will search far and wide, but Edgar will be captured and punished. He is so taken by Edmund's fidelity and loyalty that he announces that this son will be "legitimized" and thus become the heir. Edmund's conniving has served him well, more quickly than he undoubtedly expected. But before he has a chance to exult, Cornwall and Regan make their entrance.

Lines 86–129

NOTE: With their attendants in tow, note the growing importance the Duke and Duchess have taken on. The very manner of their entrance should give an idea of how grand they have become.

They dispense with the ceremony of formal greeting. They have received a report of Edgar's supposed villainy and ask for more news. Regan finds a contact point with the main story of Lear and his growing problems when she asks:

> What, did my father's godson seek your life?
> He whom my father named, your Edgar?
>
> *(lines 91–92)*

She suggests that he had been keeping bad company, carousing with Lear's retinue, and Edmund quickly confirms this. He is remarkable in his ability to determine opportunities and take advantage of them.

Regan herself is no stranger to opportunity. She uses this meeting to express her complaints against Lear and his knights that reflect the news she has received from Goneril. In fact, this is one reason why she has left home. If Lear arrives there, he will find no welcome and no comfort.

As for Cornwall, why is he impressed with Edmund's "virtue"? He welcomes Edmund to his own company, commending his "Natures of such deep trust . . . " *(line 115).*

Regan then seeks to enlist Gloucester to their cause. She has heard from both her father and her sister and claims that she seeks his counsel in deciding a course of action for her response.

Is she credible? Hasn't she already announced that she has been "well informed" by Goneril and has closed the doors of her house? Despite the sweet talk and dripping expression of old friendship, can you see Regan's true colors peeking through?

ACT II, SCENE II

Lines 1–39

Outside Gloucester's castle the two messengers meet. During the few moments they are alone on stage, we get a better and broader picture of each.

Hear what they say and watch what they do. Kent exhibits the courage, loyalty, and daring we've come to expect, and he also shows a command of rhetoric all his own. Oswald is just as true to type. As he runs from Kent's attack, you can probably picture the actor you would have playing this cowardly, sniveling role.

Lines 40–169

Oswald's cries bring the party from within the castle. Edmund draws his sword to stop Kent's onslaught, but it is Cornwall who assumes charge of the situation. As for Gloucester, he stands mute and defers to Cornwall.

Kent is identified as Lear's messenger, but Cornwall persists in trying to discover the cause of the quarrel with Oswald. Kent's replies produce nothing but a word picture of this lower-than-low creature. He defines Oswald as something made by a tailor, nothing in himself. Think of that: take away his clothes and what do you have?

What is Kent trying to do? Perhaps he thinks he can discredit Oswald's reliability as a messenger, knowing what Goneril surely would have sent to her sister.

The attempt, at any rate, fails, and Cornwall makes a decision, a judgment: Kent is to be put in the stocks for his transgression. Despite protests that he is the king's messenger and such a gesture would be disrespectful, the sentence will be executed.

Regan's vindictive disposition is heard when she echoes and adds to the sentence. Even Gloucester's plea, as he finally speaks up for mercy for the king's messenger, is put down by Cornwall, who states that he'll take that responsibility. Regan's concern is what Goneril will do when she hears that her messenger was abused.

When the Duke and Duchess of Cornwall, Edmund, and all attendants have left, Gloucester is alone with the now "stock'd" Kent, whom he does not, of course, recognize in disguise. How far they have come from the opening of the play when they were also alone on the stage.

Gloucester shows compassion for this stranger who has been harshly judged and treated, and he would go back and again ask for leniency. But Kent is stoic and claims he needs the rest! What's more, he recognizes the turns of Fortune's wheel.

Kent uses his moment of tranquility to add to our knowledge of what is taking place in the larger world. He reveals a letter from Cordelia that tells him that she is aware of the situation. (See how the image of that good creature is kept in our minds by such references. We actually haven't laid eyes on her since the very first scene.)

With a final sigh of resignation, Kent asks Fortune to smile on him and turn her wheel once more.

ACT II, SCENE III

NOTE: Obviously, Kent cannot walk offstage bound up in the stocks. But as he dozes, Shakespeare pulls our attention away from him by leading it to another commanding presence entering from an opposite side.

Edgar enters and, much like his brother before, confides in us, reveals to us his inner thoughts. Up until now he has been a pretty weak character, so easily duped that when his brother last deceived him, he could only mutter a few weak words, not even questioning what he heard.

Now he shows that he is not unimaginative and unresourceful. Having heard that he is being hunted, his picture sent about much like a "Wanted" poster today, he will do the clever thing and change his appearance, transform himself completely, at least until the heat is off.

Right before our very eyes he begins to change as he describes the lowly disguise he will assume. If Kent has turned into a peasant, Edgar goes one step further and turns into a vagrant lunatic, equivalent to the meanest hobo or "bag lady" found on the streets. They are searching for someone who is "something," but he will be "poor Tom" the beggar. He who was Edgar is now "nothing" *(line 21)*.

ACT II, SCENE IV

As Edgar drifts away, outside the social order, on the very bottom of the pile, he who should be on top enters. Still dressed in royal garments, Lear arrives outside Gloucester's castle, accompanied by a member of his entourage and the Fool.

In his very first words, Lear lets us know that there has been an abortive journey to Regan's castle. He has traveled through the night and must show the signs of such a strain.

Lines 1–59
Seeing Kent in the stocks, he asks who has done this to his messenger. When told that it was Cornwall and Regan, he shows the old fire, the old hasty judgment and rage, calling such a deed "worse than murder" *(line 22)*.

NOTE: In a previous scene we heard Oswald tell his version of the encounter. Now we hear Kent's. It's almost like reading two different newspaper reports

of something we've seen ourselves. Watch carefully
and you will discover repeated contrasts, not only
between the main plot and the subplot, but in details,
incidents, and characters.

We expect a passionate response from this easily
provoked king, but now we hear reference to the
inner part of his being that is touched by such an out-
rage. He will seek the source, and exits.

Lines 60–83

Lear's absence allows the Fool to sally with Kent,
who wants to know why Lear's entourage has been
reduced. But the Fool answers in riddles, giving a
vague warning when he talks about the rain and the
storm of what is to come. He reinforces our suspicion
that it's not always easy to tell who is the wise man
and who is the fool.

Lines 84–114

Lear returns with Gloucester, grumbling that he
has had no success producing Regan and Cornwall.
Gloucester's timid responses may be tactful, but they
are just the thing to incite Lear's further rage. And
that's exactly what happens. He spews forth curse
after curse, and then—what's this?—he pauses for a
moment and gives them the benefit of the doubt. For
the first time we hear Lear consider an alternative.
Perhaps they are ill, an acceptable excuse for not
showing up when summoned.

But, wait. The old choler triumphs, and he is back
fuming that he will not accept such a ruse. He will
break down their door if they do not show up immediately. And he sends Gloucester off with that message.

Lines 115–304

With just enough of a pause for Lear to share the
anguish of his heart, and the Fool to relieve the

mounting tension with pointed nonsense, Gloucester leads the Duke and Duchess of Cornwall onto the stage, followed by their attendants.

NOTE: As the stage begins to fill now, it is important to keep in mind a picture of how the sides are being drawn and which has the greater weight. Remember, Lear entered this scene with one attendant and the Fool. When Kent is freed, he naturally goes to Lear's side, too. Watch the opposition build.

The greetings are formal and brief. Lear gets right to the heart of the matter and pours forth his tale of Goneril's mistreatment.

But he gets little sympathy from Regan, whose polite words barely conceal the frost underneath. She takes the party line established by Goneril and indicates that she has accepted the reports of "riots" by his entourage. Lear is old, she tells him, and should defer to wiser minds. She tells him to return to Goneril and apologize.

He mocks the suggestion by kneeling and asking sarcastic forgiveness of an imaginary daughter.

Regan virtually orders him to stop his nonsense and return to her sister, but his anger is mounting. He complains that the older sister has cut his following in half, abused him verbally, and behaved like a snake. His litany of curses on Goneril is interrupted by Regan. He will, she claims, say the same of her when he is being rash.

Lear denies that; he butters her up lavishly. A trumpet is heard offstage announcing an arrival.

Oswald's entrance reminds Lear that he has not received an answer to his question of who put Kent

into the stocks. But Goneril's entrance delays an
answer. She quickly aligns herself with Regan despite
Lear's obvious displeasure.

Finally, Cornwall admits that he pronounced the
sentence on Kent. No time is given for a real reaction
from Lear, but he must guess which way the wind is
blowing. Regan pours it on by suggesting again that
he return to Goneril, but he will have none of it. In his
fiery reply he gives us a preview of coming events.

> I abjure all roofs, and choose
> To wage against the enmity o' th' air
>
> *(lines 203–4)*

He will do anything but return to this wicked daughter who has already reduced his retinue by half. He
bids Goneril an ultimate farewell, reflecting that she is
nevertheless his own child, even though she has
become corrupted. But he can do without her because
he at least has Regan.

Does he? She argues that she is not ready for him,
that she can't find provisions for his full entourage.
Besides, what does he need with so many attendants?
Why, in fact, does he need any, ask Regan and Goneril in turn. The quantitative bias is turned against
him, but Lear has a broader view. He is at the lowest
point of his fortunes as a monarch, defending himself
to his own daughters, and he can see things clearer.

What does anyone need anything for? Why are
they so richly dressed? he reminds them. Clothing
defines them.

NOTE: Keep in mind this attitude toward attire.
Costumes on stage could be very elaborate. They
could also serve as "armor" against any form of opposition. And, conversely, the lack of garments meant
exposure to any enemy or destructive force.

In a plea for sympathy, he points out his condition—"a poor old man, / As full of grief as age" *(lines 267–68)*. Will the gods allow him to sit quietly and tolerate their mistreatment? No, he will find a way to have his way.

The sound of the storm offstage punctuates the answer to his own question. Despite his grievances, he vows in the future not to show his weakness. But with a final cry as he exits, Lear shares his fear of a mental breakdown from the anguish he has experienced.

Having seen the ease with which he has mocked Goneril and played the beggar of forgiveness in front of Regan, can you totally believe Lear's appeals for sympathy here? Is it perhaps overindulgence in self-pity? Or is it the real thing?

The stiff-lipped daughters show how determined they are after Lear has left. Gloucester tells them that a fierce storm is brewing outside, but they don't care. Let him stay out there and learn his lesson. He's brought it all on himself, they agree, as they order Gloucester to leave Lear outside, and Cornwall gives the order to bar the door.

Even if you grant that there is some truth in what they have said, how much can you sympathize with Goneril and Regan when you hear their version of the facts? The lines that draw their portraits grow heavier as their evil natures gradually emerge.

ACT III
ACT III, SCENE I

On the other hand, Kent's character is firmly fixed and will not vary. (Note that he is useful in many ways to the playwright. Again Shakespeare exploits his function as "news bulletin" reporter to clear the stage and prepare for the passion of the scene to come.) It is too soon to appreciate the change in Lear as he contends "with the fretful elements" *(line 4)*, but a report of this behavior sets us up for what is to come.

The political situation is reviewed, too. We learn that there is underground activity between Cornwall and Albany, each of whom would like to run the whole show. But the unrest has produced a response from France that shows that interest still active. Indeed, French forces are reported to have landed in England and Kent would have them made aware of the king's current situation. He sends the king's courtier off to bear that message and adds a few words of his own for Cordelia. She will recognize him by the ring he sends.

Again Cordelia is recalled and reinforced as "goodness" striving against opposing forces. She has been absent from the stage, but have you forgotten what she represents? Is there a need to think any more about her pride? Her stubbornness? Just look at how she is absolved in absentia.

ACT III, SCENE II

NOTE: Here is the first great storm scene of *King Lear*. To get full value, to make its dramatic effect profound on audiences then and now, it took more than the sound of thunder offstage. It would take the powerful effects of speech and movement. The rhetoric thunder in Lear's words is undoubtedly greater and more moving than the artificial, but the combination must have been stunning. Properly acted, in these scenes the storm and Lear become united in force and fury.

As the storm rages, Lear enters with the Fool. What a difference from any of his previous entrances! Gone are the stately procession, the court attendants, the regal trappings. Only the Fool, the loyal court jester, is with him to mitigate the tremendous agony of Lear's burden. Joining the voice of the storm with his own voice of protest, Lear calls on the celestial powers to bring down the full force of the tempest against his two ungrateful daughters. Let them be the messengers of his revenge.

In another voice, calm yet impassioned, he asks the gods to witness his woeful condition.

When Kent arrives on the scene, he joins the Fool in a plea to bring Lear in to some kind of shelter. But Lear is still full of his inner turmoil and will not be moved. He continues to rant against the tyrannies of his enemies. Lear acknowledges himself as somewhat responsible, but he is "More sinned against than sinning." *(line 60)*.

Kent's entreaties finally make their point and Lear, recognizing that he has been carried away by the storm and his own anger, suddenly notices the cold and the rain. Taking pity on the Fool, who has suffered from the elements along with him, he enters the hovel Kent has found. The Fool shares with the audience a paradoxical prophecy of the greater storm to come:

> Then shall the realm of Albion
> Come to great confusion.
>
> *(lines 91–92)*

NOTE: Albion (another name for England) will also suffer the turn of Fortune's wheel and feel the trauma created by the inversion, the power struggle, and all the chaos unleashed by the "unnatural acts" we are witnessing.

ACT III, SCENE III

It's scoundrel time once again. The Gloucester/Edmund/Edgar subplot begins to accelerate.

As Gloucester and Edmund appear on stage, the father confesses to his illegitimate son that he does not like the "unnatural" behavior of Cornwall and Regan; an upsetting of order has resulted from their assumption of authority in his house, with the guests ruling the host. Hypocritical Edmund is quick to agree that it is indeed "savage and unnatural." But wasn't this the very thing he expressed a desire to do in the forged letter—if we assume that it represented his own wishes?

Gloucester makes the mistake of confiding that he has received a letter that presumably comes from sympathizers with the French invaders who are already mounting their forces somewhere in the land. The old earl plans to disobey Cornwall's orders and go to the king with such relief and comforts as he can provide. Gloucester asks Edmund to cover for him by saying that he is unwell and has retired for the evening. He'll take the risk under penalty of death for the sake of the master he has served faithfully.

Once Gloucester leaves, the treacherous Edmund reveals that he will betray this confidence to advance his own cause.

In this short scene, two character studies are engraved a little deeper as the tension builds.

ACT III, SCENE IV

The scene shifts back to the storm. You may wonder why it didn't just continue uninterrupted, since there doesn't seem to be a time change. Some modern productions attempt to run the storm scenes all together and they generally run into the problem Shakespeare avoided by separating them.

The intensity is so great and the passions are so tremendous that it is impossible to rise higher, or even to sustain the pitch. It takes all the playwright's skill to combine prose and poetry, song snatches, rhymes, even nonsense, to maintain the texture of these scenes and create the dynamics. Don't miss the sound of the words as you pay attention to their meaning; you are hearing an exquisite symphony of emotion and excitement, filled with crescendos as well as peaceful interludes.

Lines 1–27

At the doorway to shelter, Kent begs Lear to enter. But the old king gives a calm analysis of why he is not bothered by the wind and the rain. How can it compare with the turmoil within his mind and body? He knows that he has been mistreated by his daughters, who have turned him out in such a night; he knows how fierce the weather is. He sends the Fool inside; he will follow in a moment. First he wishes to pray.

Lines 28–36

In a supreme moment of introspection and exposure of his deepest understanding, Lear reflects on the earthly condition of his fellow suffering human beings. The other "poor naked wretches" (line 28) who have no shelter arouse a compassion we haven't seen before in him, and it inspires—compels—our sympathy. As he reveals an ability to care for others under such devastating circumstances as the storm and his own exile, we begin to care for him.

Lear even shows an understanding of how clothing determines the social order and shields us from a true

vision of man's condition. When he says, "Take phys-
ic, pomp" *(line 33)*, we know that he is reminding
himself of his own past errors.

Lines 37–107

The breakdown that has been threatening now
occurs when Edgar, disguised as poor Tom o' Bedlam, comes out and opens an escape hatch from
Lear's world of sorrows to the safer world of madness.

Edgar plays the part of lunatic wanderer to the hilt
and quickly becomes Lear's sounding board and
counterfoil to repeated complaints of his daughters'
ingratitude. Positioning the madman as a learned philosopher, Lear thrusts at him with questions the play
itself is asking:

Is man no more than this?

(lines 97–98)

What is the cause of thunder?

(line 146)

We can see that Lear has now embarked on a voy-
age of discovery through the darkness in which his
mind is wandering. In streaks of light and insight, he
indicates new awareness. When he sees Edgar's
wretched rags, he begins to take off his own clothes to
identify with this creature of the lowest social order.

Lines 108–175

Even Gloucester's arrival cannot stop the progress
Lear is making. And Gloucester's own blindness, his
failure to recognize his own son—even granting that
he is disguised—underscores the contrast of Lear's
growing vision.

NOTE: Things are not what they seem. The more
Lear appears mad, the more he is perceived so by

Gloucester and Kent. But the more he is learning within his suffering heart and mind.

Gloucester, the prosaic, patient, well-meaning soul, rises a bit in our estimation by his attempt to be of assistance. But there's irony in his acknowledgment of Lear's driven condition provoked by his daughters, and his comparison of his own betrayal by his legitimate son. How ironic is his cry, "The grief hath crazed my wits" (line 161), in view of Lear's madness and sorrow.

As the storm rages outside, the group moves inward to shelter and momentary relief.

ACT III, SCENE V

Here is another break from the compelling passion of Lear's growing madness and the dark shadows surrounding him. We are given a close-up view of the utmost villainy at work. It is not enough for us to know that Edmund will betray his father; we get to witness it in this "meanwhile, back at the castle" interlude.

Having heard the news of Gloucester's "disloyalty," Cornwall acknowledges that Edgar might have been justified in wishing to have his father put away. As Edmund sighs and beats his breast at the pain he suffers in turning in his father, Cornwall gives him the happy news that a reward is at hand. As far as this "worthy arch and patron" (Act II, Scene i, line 59) is concerned, Edmund is now the Earl of Gloucester.

Just listen to the hypocrisy that abounds in this scene as Edmund and Cornwall glibly toss off references to "loyalty" and "trust" and "love." If you didn't know better by now, wouldn't this sound like the most sincere conversation you could imagine? Since you have the facts behind it in your mind, how powerful is its "villainy" manifest?

ACT III, SCENE VI

As Lear stumbles down the road to darkest despair and madness, there are telltale moments of lucidity and passion. Having touched us with sublime humility and fiery anguish, we now witness the debasement of the monarch—the highest court of appeal at one time—as he indulges in a grotesque parody of the court of law.

Lines 6–83

Gloucester and Kent have managed to gather the three unbridled spirits and have brought Lear, Edgar, and the Fool into a shelter, perhaps a cottage.

NOTE: Picture the three of them prancing about the stage. Edgar is spouting gibberish to maintain his disguise as "poor Tom"; the Fool is trying to entertain his master, to alleviate the pain of his suffering with riddles; and Lear is mainly in the darkness of his tortured mind, but emerges now and then to give telling replies to the Fool's riddles.

With Gloucester gone to seek further comforts, Lear decides to hold a "trial" to judge his daughters' evil behavior. He appoints the "mad" Edgar as judge, the Fool as a member of the jury, and he will prosecute. With a stool standing in for the accused, he declares Goneril guilty of kicking "the poor King her father" (lines 47–48). Did we see this happen? Or can we accept it as an accurate metaphor for his treatment at her hands?

Regan is similarly accused, but the trial breaks down as Lear's mind turns to self-pity. He sees light long enough to tell those assembled that Regan's heart should be examined to see if there is any "natural" cause for the evil it contains.

But the madness is growing in him even as he grows calmer. For a moment he thinks that Edgar is one of his hundred knights, though strangely costumed. Isn't this an ironic fulfillment of Regan's earlier accusation?

At last he is persuaded to retire for the evening and goes to lie down. Perhaps thinking he is back in his own castle, he gives orders for the curtains to be drawn and supper, the evening meal, to be served in the morning.

To that the Fool replies: "And I'll go to bed at noon" (line 83). These are the Fool's last spoken words; after this scene he disappears. Why Shakespeare did this is one of the great questions, a subject of much critical speculation. You have seen the Fool in action. You have seen the function he served. Now you must decide how much of a loss he really is. Do you believe he could continue to provide any comfort for his master whose madness, if not his anger, has been relatively calm up to this point?

NOTE: It has been suggested that the Fool's line can be interpreted to mean that he will die now, at the zenith of his life. Do you believe this? If not, what other explanation can you offer for this, his final statement?

Lines 90–113

The trusted Kent, who has witnessed all this, assures the returned Gloucester that Lear's "wits are gone." But Gloucester has even worse news to report. He has overheard a plot to kill the king. They must clear out and take Lear to Dover, where he will be safe. (There, in the southeast of England, the French forces have landed.) Kent bemoans the fact that the rest Lear needed so desperately to help cure him of his madness is obviously not at hand.

The faithful Gloucester, Kent, and the Fool literally carry Lear away, much as he virtually departs from the mainstream of the action now. The wheels set in motion by his initial act and by Gloucester's misplacement of trust are now spinning furiously and will carry matters forward.

Edgar lingers for a moment to call the audience's attention to the pathetic nature of the scene they have witnessed, and to remind us that "Who alone suffers suffers most i' the mind" *(line 102)*. It is a sad omen of what we are yet to see.

ACT III, SCENE VII

NOTE: The widely discussed violence of today's television and movies has nothing on the brutality of this scene, which is performed live before the audience. However, it is not gratuitous. It belongs, it is integral, and we are ready for it. Shakespeare needed an act of compelling intensity to prepare us for the greater catastrophe that Lear will experience: this physical act of violence serves that purpose. And what else could compare to the towering ferocity of the storm, the tumult of Lear's madness, and the manic insanity of the disguised Edgar? Would a mild reproach, a slap on the wrist, be enough? Kent was put into the stocks for simply drawing his sword on a servant; Gloucester's punishment must fit his crime, and it must be witnessed.

Lines 1–25

As soon as Cornwall has sent Goneril off to bring Albany up to date on the French invasion, he orders a search for "the traitor Gloucester" *(line 3)*.

Like two harpies, the sisters call for punishment.
Regan suggests hanging, but Goneril, who once told
Lear that she loved him "Dearer than eyesight" (*Act I,
Scene i, line 56*), cries: "Pluck out his eyes" (*line 5*). In
this case, it is his sister-in-law's counsel that Cornwall
will follow.

Lines 27–107

But before such sentence can be executed, justice
will be mocked again. Gloucester is brought in and a
hurried inquisition is held. He must suffer the indignation and torture of his accusers' abuse. As Regan
plucks the old man's beard, we hear her echo a former
accusation: "So white, and such a traitor! (*line 35*).

Regan and Cornwall are determined to discover
what they can before punishing Gloucester. They can
hardly believe—or perhaps don't want to believe—
the news that the king has been sent off to Dover.
Why would Gloucester point him in that direction? In
an ironic and sad preview of his fate, he tells them,

> Because I would not see thy cruel nails
> Pluck out his poor old eyes; . . .
>
> (*lines 56–57*)

With that preparation, it is not surprising to see
Cornwall execute the punishment, to see him physically put out Gloucester's eyes. Still, the horror is
there, and to underscore it one servant tries to stop
Cornwall. He engages the duke in a duel, but Regan
rises to the challenge and runs a sword through the
servant's back. Cornwall crawls toward the comple-
tion of Gloucester's punishment and puts out his second eye.

The blinded earl now begs for the comfort of his son
Edmund and receives another form of punishment
when Regan tells him that it was Edmund who
betrayed him.

In his agony, Gloucester recognizes his former metaphoric blindness, which led him to cast Edgar out into the cold.

In the ultimate revelation of her savage disposition, Regan punctuates the cruelty we've just witnessed by ordering a servant to throw the bleeding Gloucester out "and let him smell / His way to Dover" *(lines 92–93)*.

When he is gone, Regan discovers that Cornwall has been injured in his duel with the servant, and leads him offstage.

The extent of the wickedness is not lost on the observers on stage or on those in the audience. The remaining servants share our sympathy and compassion for Gloucester. They agree to give him medicines to ease his physical suffering but, as they indicate, only heaven can really help him now.

ACT IV

ACT IV, SCENE I

There is only brief relief from the horror just witnessed. In this scene Gloucester returns to the stage; his role becomes—like Lear's—essentially passive from now on. But at the same time, the emotional appeals that Shakespeare will direct through both these old men will also grow more powerful.

Lines 1–9
Edgar, still disguised, enters and reminds us that his lot in life is the lowest. He is, he says, at his very worst.

Lines 10–79
Gloucester stumbles in, aided by an old family retainer. When the blind earl tries to dismiss his ser-

vant, he is reminded that he cannot see his way. What does Gloucester reply?

> I have no way, and therefore want no eyes;
>   I stumbled when I saw: . . .
>
> *(lines 18–19)*

Discovering his father in this condition and hearing his pathetic revelation, his plea to find his lost son, Edgar is in agony. Now Edgar realizes that there is no such thing as "worst." There is always more.

NOTE: Why doesn't Edgar just own up to who he really is? It wouldn't serve the play's development, but how can such an opportunity go by? Watch what happens and see if you can detect a reason to continue his disguise.

Gloucester recognizes the voice of the beggar he had met the night before, and mentions that ironically he was reminded of his son. Just another trick of fate, he comments, as he makes the most pessimistic observation of the play:

> As flies to wanton boys, are we to th' gods,
>   They kill us for their sport.
>
> *(lines 36–37)*

Is that the ultimate "message" of the play? Is that the answer to everything that has happened and will happen? Or is man himself the determining factor for both good and evil? There is no cut-and-dried answer, but there are, as always, clues.

NOTE: The Wheel of Fortune has come around for Gloucester, much as it did for Edgar moments ago. It's natural for the old man to bemoan his fate. Recognition is important, but remember, the wheel is never stationary. It continues to move, and Gloucester has other discoveries yet to make.

The nonrecognition scene continues: it serves the drama for Edgar to remain unknown to his father. To make that acceptable, Shakespeare contrives a purpose. The old servant is let go and Gloucester now comes to depend on the beggar. Aware of his wretched condition, the earl wishes to provide him with clothes, to make him more "respectable" as relief from his suffering. In an obvious gesture of Christian charity Gloucester gives away his purse.

He asks the beggar if he is familiar with the Dover coast and the cliffs found there.

NOTE:　　One of the best-known features of the English landscape, this would strike a familiar note with the audience. It would also suggest what Gloucester has in mind. Imagine a character in a play today saying, "Take me to the Brooklyn Bridge." It wouldn't be too difficult to figure out what he was planning.

Edgar answers affirmatively. Gloucester asks to be led there and brought to the edge where ". . . from that place / I shall no leading need" (lines 77–78). Why wait for the gods? He will create his own destiny. Edgar takes his arm, and they depart.

This new twist of the subplot, leading it toward the main plot, serves another purpose. Have you noticed how Edgar has begun to gain importance? He has not yet initiated action, but his role as participant—and as gradual hero—constantly grows from here on.

ACT IV, SCENE II

A fresh complication of the main plot takes place, too, as new intrigue begins. The web being spun by the wicked daughters and the equally evil Edmund is developing knots. The pregnant suggestion of a rift between the forces of Albany and Cornwall is only one of the problems.

Lines 1–28

The first breach occurs as Goneril arrives home with Edmund at her side. She hears from Oswald, the faithful, fawning steward, that Albany has heard of the French landing in England, but it has not aroused him. Told of Gloucester's supposed treachery and Edmund's supposed loyalty, he was even less pleased.

Recognizing a problem in the making, Goneril sends Edmund off to rejoin Cornwall's forces as she professes her great passion for this earl-presumptive, sealing it with a kiss. Edmund hides behind a chivalrous farewell that tells us nothing of his true feelings for her.

Lines 29–68

Albany enters and we quickly see how he feels about Goneril and her recent actions. He recognizes her and her sister as "Tigers, not daughters," whose gross treatment of their father will not go unpunished. He, too, observes that the gods will not allow such offenses to continue—otherwise, chaos would result.

divine intervention

Goneril, not unlike Lear in his earlier rash state, lashes out at him and calls him a coward. He sees her as nothing but a beast.

NOTE: Remember where animals stood then in
the "natural order." Not only were they at the bottom, they had their own ranking: at the very lowest
are "monsters," the embodiment of evil.

Lines 69–98

A messenger interrupts this verbal battle to inform
them of the death of the Duke of Cornwall from his
recent wound. At the same time, Albany hears of
Gloucester's blinding by his brother-in-law and the
servant's attempt to intercede. In the final result,
Albany sees justice served by the vengeful gods;
Cornwall was punished swiftly for his heinous act.

Goneril is given a letter from her sister, who she
realizes is now a widow and possible contender for
Edmund. As she goes to draft a suitable reply, Albany
learns that Edmund had come to the palace with Goneril and turned right around. Moreover, Edmund's
betrayal of his father had led to the vile punishment.

In a final impassioned statement, Albany vows
revenge, to finish himself what the gods have apparently only partially done.

The softer shades are disappearing from the palette
as the evil characters grow blacker and the good ones
lighter. Is there any room for doubt about Goneril
now? And what about Albany? From here on we
know what to expect of them.

Still we have to ask, why doesn't Albany join up
with the forces against Regan and Edmund and even
Goneril? Why doesn't he go over to the "good guys"?
Could it be that he is reluctant to become involved in a
civil war? Or does patriotism make him feel he must
defend the country against foreigners? Albany is in a

difficult position. It will be interesting to see how Shakespeare deals with the problem.

ACT IV, SCENE III

It's time for another news bulletin, a report by Kent and an anonymous gentleman.

We learn that although the French have landed, the King of France has returned home to deal with an urgent problem there. This easy removal of a problem here may strike you as a bit clumsy, but look what it sets up.

With France gone, we identify Cordelia as the virtual head of the invasion. That's not as bad as the possibility of foreigners beating the English in battle. We can root for Cordelia and her army, Lear, and the "good guys."

Kent is told of Cordelia's reaction to the news of her father's situation. She grows even more virtuous in our eyes. (Remember, we have not seen Cordelia since the very first scene.)

Like just about everyone else, Kent looks to the heavens to discover the rulers of man's fate. How could three such different daughters be produced by the same parent?

Kent tells us that Lear is now in Dover. In lucid moments, the mad king remembers his harsh judgment of Cordelia and is now too ashamed to go to her. Kent will lead the gentleman to Lear to do the job of persuasion, while he attends to other matters.

ACT IV, SCENE IV

When we last saw Cordelia, she was leaving in disgrace. Now, as Queen of France, she enters with drums, fanfare, attendants, and all the splendor of her position. What a sight, and what a reward for our patience.

NOTE: This is the first we see, too, of those
French forces we've been hearing about. If we are to
believe that there is a battle brewing, we need some
demonstration of a worthy foe. The grand entrance to
this scene does just that.

We have high hopes for Cordelia, and we are not
disappointed. Her very first words show compassion
and concern for her father. She describes the report
she has received of his appearance, dressed with
roadside weeds as he wanders about madly singing
away.

Cordelia asks a doctor if there is any hope. Is Lear
too far gone? Can he be cured? The doctor's answer is
brief. Rest and the healing power of "nature" are the
only things that might be effective. Cordelia vows to
find Lear and provide that relief.

Told that the British forces are getting closer, she
resumes her role as leader of the French but joins her
cause to her father's. In a firm statement she lets us
know that the only purpose of this invasion is the
restoration of Lear's throne to him. This is important—it gives us even greater justification for cheering
on her side.

ACT IV, SCENE V

The nonmilitary conflict is heating up, too. Regan
has received Goneril's messenger, Oswald, and is told
that Albany is preparing his troops, even though
Goneril "is the better soldier" *(line 3)*.

But Regan is more concerned about Edmund. She
tries to find out what is going on between him and her
sister. Oswald, however, is uncooperative: he will not
show her Goneril's letter to Edmund that he is carrying.

Regan goes so far as to tell Oswald that she is better suited, being a widow, to marry Edmund. There is no question of this woman's lust and passion for that evil man.

She gives Oswald a sign of her devotion to pass along to Edmund when he meets him. Moreover, should Oswald come across Gloucester, the vindictive Regan offers a reward for killing that traitor.

Oswald accepts the commission, and departs.

ACT IV, SCENE VI

After the interplay of two villains, each outdoing the other in hypocritical protest of sincere intention, the scene shifts to Edgar's gentle treatment of Gloucester.

Lines 1–80

Edgar convinces his father by word pictures that they have arrived at their destination. He leads him to the supposed edge of the cliff and stands aside while the old man prepares to make his final peace.

Gloucester gives away his last earthly goods, and consigns his fate to the higher powers. He could not go on without losing faith in the gods. With a final blessing on his lost son, he throws himself forward and faints.

NOTE: For all its pathos, the moment is also funny. The two-foot fall and the subsequent dialogue are lighter than anything we've had since the Fool departed. It's not broad comedy, but it does provide some relief from the heaviness of the tragedy that is building steadily. Simply because you're observing a grand tragedy, don't reject the value of comic elements. A little laughter will clear the air and pave the way for the tears later.

At the same time, it's worth comparing Gloucester's route with Lear's "journey" of despair. Gloucester has chosen suicide; Lear goes mad. Is one worse
than the other?

Edgar convinces Gloucester that he is alive and that
a miracle has occurred. Ironically, a man-made miracle has: the blind earl has regained hope and faith. He
doesn't know that all this has been his son's doing,
and Edgar perpetuates the deception by assuring him
that ". . . the clearest gods . . . have preserved thee"
(lines 73–74). That's good enough for Gloucester. He
vows to suffer his affliction without complaint until he
comes to a natural end.

Lines 80–199

We have not seen Lear for some time, although we
have had a recent description of his condition. Now
he enters and fits the description to the letter. He is
covered with weeds, a "natural" king. There are
traces of his former bearing and authority, but there is
even greater humility.

Lear tells us that he knows he was surrounded by
poor advisers when he was the absolute monarch.
Then his clothing and royal trappings kept him from
seeing true conditions. Now he has learned, he has
gained vision and can suffer pain.

Gloucester recognizes the voice. It is the king.

"Ay, every inch a king" *(line 106),* replies Lear, who
then begins a mad discourse in which he links lust
and adultery to the violence that has taken place. Hidden in his mad prattling are tremendous insights, but
also anger and resignation.

The pathetic scene of the madman, Lear, and the
blind man, Gloucester, continues with the earl showing his continued devotion to his master. Lear offers a
topsy-turvy commentary on his condition, which

lands right side up every now and then. He knows
the difference between his former condition as "something" and his present state as "nothing." He knows
the difference between fancy clothes that hide villains,
and nakedness that sometimes shows true worth. He
does not want to seem to be what he isn't and he
starts to undress.

Lear recognizes Gloucester, and he offers his own
eyes to the blind earl. In his philosophical outlook,
Lear can see that we create our own misfortunes. This
is a bleak outlook. Why shouldn't " . . . we cry that we
are come / To this great stage of fools" *(lines 179–80)*,
he asks before he is overcome by his madness and
turns to thoughts of revenge. He knows his enemy,
including his sons-in-law, whom he would " . . . kill,
kill, kill, kill, kill, kill!" *(line 184)*.

Lear sees himself as "The natural fool of fortune"
(line 188). He compares his bodily pain to his mental
anguish as madness again seizes him. With attendants in pursuit, this sad, tortured creature runs off,
babbling.

Lines 200–281
One of Cordelia's men tells Edgar that the battle will
soon take place, but the queen, Cordelia, will stay
right there until her father is brought to her.

Gloucester repeats his vow to stay alive. For now,
Edgar will find some shelter for him.

But first Oswald comes upon them. His immediate
thought is for his "fortune," the reward Regan
offered. Not only that, but Oswald believes he will
rise in everyone's opinion if he slays this enemy.

But Oswald has not reckoned with the real Edgar
behind the beggar's rags, who mocks the steward in a
peasant's voice. He even uses a peasant's weapon,
some sort of cudgel, to mortally wound the preten-
tious steward.

In a single gesture of decency before he dies, Oswald asks his opponent to deliver the letters he carries to "Edmund Earl of Gloucester." The impact of that declaration must have shaken both Edgar and his father. Just as important is the precedent set by this villain's dying act of goodness. We can expect to find it repeated in this play with its constant parallels.

Edgar reads the letter. He learns that Goneril has pledged herself to Edmund and hopes that the battle will take care of the problem of her present husband. If not, Edmund will have to rescue her in the only way possible.

But Edgar has developed his own sense of cunning, and he saves the letter for use as ammunition later. When the time comes, he'll take care of Goneril and serve his own interests.

As drums signal the battle approaching, Edgar leads the sorrowing Gloucester away as the old man laments the king's madness and his own grief.

ACT IV, SCENE VII

At long last, we see Cordelia reunited with her father. It is certainly an emotional scene, but it's more than a play for sympathy. As it unfolds, notice how carefully each step is taken, a striking contrast from the opening, banishment scene.

Lines 1–43

Cordelia's gentle nature and essential goodness are on display as she discusses with both Kent and the doctor Lear's condition. She is told that the king has slept long enough to risk waking him. Try to remember her posture in the opening scene. Questions of stubbornness, conniving, and the like melt away as she proceeds toward the moment of reunion.

Lines 44–97

To the accompaniment of gentle music and Cordelia's kiss, Lear awakens. At first he thinks he has died
and gone to heaven or purgatory. Is this another miracle, like Gloucester's? He thinks that Cordelia is a
spirit and, to the audience, she must indeed appear
so.

Gradually he comes to his senses and he knows
that he is in the presence of the daughter he has
wronged. He kneels before her in a penitent gesture,
but she asks him to rise and give her his benedic-
tion.

Lear's return to sanity is evident as he acknowledges that he is "a very foolish fond old man" *(line 60)*.
He knows that he is not completely out of the woods,
but he can identify Cordelia.

Riveting the audience by the concentration of kind-
ness taking place on the stage, Lear admits that he has
wronged Cordelia, but she rebuffs the suggestion.
Total reconciliation is at hand.

Lear is so humbled that all he can do is repeat that
he is old and foolish, as the shining heroine, whom he
always loved most, leads him off to further rest.

Moved by the scene he has witnessed, Kent prepares to join the fighting forces. He is told, meanwhile, that Cornwall is dead and that Edmund has
taken his place at the head of Cornwall's troops. It is
rumored that Edgar has vanished and was seen with
the Earl of Kent in Germany! We might welcome this
touch of irony as a bit of relief after the heavy senti-
ment just experienced on the stage.

Wearied from his struggles to support Lear and act
as the needed go-between, Kent departs to face whatever the battle will decide.

ACT V

ACT V, SCENE I

The long-awaited battle is about to take place. During the final moments of preparation for the British forces, Edmund strides forward, very much the master of the situation.

Lines 1–17

Edmund sends an officer to see what's happening with Albany's troops. Regan is more concerned with another situation: she tries to get Edmund to assure her of his faithfulness to her and his disinterest in Goneril. Her jealousy and desperation are apparent. Edmund gives her his pledge as Albany and Goneril enter with their troops.

NOTE: The two sides are again lined up on the stage, with Edmund somewhere between or perhaps traveling back and forth. Once more the arrangement of characters on the stage tells part of the story.

Lines 18–37

The depth of Goneril's lust for Edmund is revealed in an aside as they enter. She would rather lose the battle than lose her lover to her sister.

Albany uses this opportunity to clarify his position. He tells us that he fights to repel the French invaders, not to oppose the king. The three villains—Edmund, Regan, and Goneril—can hardly agree with him fast enough.

As they are dispersing to take care of final arrangements, Regan manipulates Goneril into coming with her to her tent, despite the older sister's awareness of the discussion that awaits her there.

Lines 38–68

As Albany lingers for a moment, Edgar, still disguised as a beggar, enters and asks for a word. Now is the time to turn over Goneril's treacherous letter to Edmund. He does so, but before Albany is allowed to open it, Edgar extracts a promise. He asks to be allowed to produce a champion to prove the truth of the letter.

NOTE: The rules of chivalry come into play here. Apparently, an accusation such as the one against Edmund could be challenged and decided by a duel with someone of equivalent rank. Even though he is unknown to Albany, Edgar has obviously piqued his interest enough to obtain his promise.

Edgar and Albany leave; Edmund appears alone on the stage. We learn that he has been, as we might expect, two-faced in his relationships with Goneril and Regan: he has sworn faithfulness to each. He'll let the battle decide if Goneril will become a widow and then he'll choose between them.

As for Lear and Cordelia, if they are captured, he has no intention of letting them live.

In these last moments before the battle, our questions about any of the characters in the drama should have been answered.

ACT V, SCENE II

In terms of spoken words, this is the shortest scene in the play. What takes place, however, is a strong thrust to Fortune's wheel.

With the sound of battle music playing in the distance, drums and colors accompany Cordelia, arm in arm with Lear, followed by her troops, as they cross through and depart for the battle.

A moment later, Edgar takes his father by the arm. He is leading Gloucester to peace, in contrast to Cordelia's unhappy mission. Securing a quiet place by a tree, he departs for the action on the field.

From offstage we hear the sounds of military horns sounding the charge, sounds of battle and, finally, retreat.

NOTE: From the brief period of time devoted to it, we can tell that the actual military conflict offstage is not as important as the events that led up to it on stage. We will see the results shortly.

Edgar returns to tell Gloucester that the French forces have lost. Lear and Cordelia have been taken prisoner. They themselves must flee to avoid capture.

Gloucester's courage appears to desert him, but Edgar reminds him that the wheel can still spin in any direction. He still believes that it is the gods who decide these things and he trusts to fate.

ACT V, SCENE III

A work of the magnitude of *King Lear* demands a truly grand finale. Shakespeare has tantalized us by leaving all the loose ends dangling. And, except for Cornwall's premature death and the subvillain Oswald's dispatch to the netherworld, all the characters are still on hand. The good ones are capable of heroic acts; the villains await their just desserts.

Lines 1–25

A procession of grand proportions, equal to or greater even than Lear's first entrance, takes place as Edmund marches onto the stage, followed by his troops and the captive Lear and Cordelia.

His first act is to order the captives taken away to detention until their fate is decided. But before they leave, Cordelia confesses that she is saddened at this turn of Fortune's wheel, not so much for herself as for her father. But Lear does not share her view. He offers her a picture of prison as a welcome retreat from the cares they have recently shared. That they may face death doesn't enter into the picture of the happy life he paints for her. He is calm and perhaps still a little mad when he tells her that they will have nothing to do but watch the rise and fall of the "great ones" *(line 18)*.

Lines 26–39

The minute they are gone, Edmund calls one of his officers into his confidence. A commission is given. It is the order to do away with the prisoners before they are formally judged and condemned.

Lines 40–106

As the officer leaves, a trumpet announces the entrance of Albany, Goneril, Regan, and more troops.

Albany has apparently read Goneril's love letter to Edmund, which he received from the disguised Edgar. But before he deals with that, he calls for the captives. When Edmund tells him that they are in custody, Albany rebukes him for his presumption in making that decision.

Now Regan steps forward and informs everyone that Edmund is acting on her authority. When that authority is challenged, the two sisters snarl at each other. They begin to fight over Edmund, although Regan confesses that she is feeling ill.

It doesn't matter, Albany tells them. In fact, he accuses Edmund of treason and names Goneril as his accessory. Unaware that Edmund's title is not really merited or secure, Albany extends to him the courtesy of a chivalrous defense and orders the trumpets to announce the call for a champion to challenge Edmund.

NOTE: The complicated rules of chivalry demand that the rank of the challenger be no lower than that of the defendant. In other words, you don't prove anything if you beat someone less "worthy." Is that really any different from today? Modern weapons are more sophisticated, but the value system has endured.

Regan cries out that she is indeed sick, and Goneril in an aside lets us know that she has administered the cause. As Edmund puts on a show of bravado, Regan is led offstage to Albany's tent.

Lines 107–151
A herald enters and reads the challenge. The trumpet is sounded three times and Edgar, armed and disguised, enters to present his qualifications. Without identifying himself, he claims nobility equal to his opponent. He accuses Edmund of crimes against the gods, against his father and his brother, against Albany; he calls Edmund a traitor from head to toe and vows to prove it in combat with him.

Edmund is so confident of himself that he accepts the challenge of his anonymous opponent. They fight. Edmund loses and is fatally wounded, but he does not die instantly.

Lines 152–222
Goneril rages at this trick that has cost her her lover. Albany silences her by flaunting her "love note" at her accusingly. Sneering at him and his charges, she rushes offstage. Seeing her desperation, Albany sends one of his officers to keep an eye on her.

As Edmund lies dying, he asks the identity of his opponent and acknowledges that the accusations were indeed true. Edgar, rapidly growing in heroic stature, identifies himself and offers some philosophic views on this outcome. He doesn't accept the gods as fickle—they are just. Something of a prig, he does sound a bit tactless when he attributes Gloucester's punishment to the adulterous act that produced Edmund.

But Edmund hasn't the strength for debate as he lies dying. He agrees, noting that "The wheel is come full circle" *(line 175)*.

Albany welcomes Edgar, who tells him his recent history—how he came upon Gloucester and cared for him and never revealed himself until recently. Has this been some sort of penance? Some "mortification of the flesh" to ennoble Edgar further in our minds?

Edgar's final act of revelation came just as Gloucester came to his own end, dying between the contrasting emotions of joy and grief.

Edgar also reveals that he had come across Kent during the battle and discovered the service he had performed for Lear.

Lines 223–257

An attendant bursts in, shouting and clutching a bloody knife in his hand. Goneril has confessed to poisoning her sister, and has killed herself. The irony of the death of his two fiancées and his own doom is not lost on Edmund.

Another voice of impending death is heard as Kent enters "To bid my king and master aye good night" *(line 235)*. This reminds Albany of Cordelia and Lear. Where has Edmund sent them?

As the bodies of Goneril and Regan are brought out, Edmund is prompted to do a good deed. He

reveals that he has given a written order for the death
of Lear and Cordelia but he has changed his mind. As
an officer hurries off toward the prisoners, Edmund
describes the commission he had given with Goneril's
agreement: Cordelia was to be hanged and blamed as
a suicide. The dying Edmund is then carried off.

Lines 238–327

Why has Edmund delayed revealing his plot
against the captives? Did it take the sight of the dead
Goneril and Regan to prompt him to act "Despite of
[his] own nature"? Any credit he might receive in
heaven fades in an instant as Lear now enters with the
dead Cordelia in his arms.

The heartrending scene of reconciliation between
father and estranged daughter was only a preview of
the sorrow we now witness. Lear is powerful and yet
pitiful in his anguish as he croons over Cordelia's
body. Grasping at the tiniest hope, he calls for a mir-
ror to see if he can detect the faintest breath. Even a
feather. If it stirs, there is a chance. But she is gone
and Lear can claim only the joy of having avenged her
death by killing her murderer.

Kent is acknowledged, but no attempt is made to
separate Lear from the body of Cordelia, still cradled
in his arms.

A messenger enters and announces that Edmund is
dead, but to Albany this is a trifle. The duke declares
that he may have won the battle, but he restores absolute power to the rightful monarch, Lear.

But there is not much time left for Lear. His final
words are on his tongue as he looks to Cordelia's lips
for an indication of life. Who can forget how earlier he
looked to her lips for an indication of her love?

The very simplicity, the short, one-syllable words of
this last speech show how weak he has become. But
he is hopeful to the last.

Do you see this? Look on her. Look, her lips,
Look there, look there.

(lines 311–12)

Lear dies.

NOTE: What does he see? Critics have argued
this point endlessly. There is really no valid answer
but your own. If you view the play as pessimistic, you
will see a dark vision through Lear's dying gaze. But if
you find optimism in its conclusion, you will see a
happier sight. Maybe the truth lies somewhere
between and, like Gloucester, Lear has died between
the two extremes of joy and grief.

Crying that perhaps Lear has only fainted, Edgar
rushes to his side, but Kent stops him. Do not disturb
his final rest. Lear has suffered enough.

With Lear gone, Albany relinquishes the responsibility for ruling England to Kent and Edgar, but Kent
refuses. He has borne the weight of too much sorrow
and will indeed soon follow his master.

Edgar acknowledges in somber tones that we have
all learned from the tragedy we have witnessed. Now
we can only take up the burden of future survival.

Lear and his daughters all lie dead on the stage,
surrounded by his nobles and the army that was really always his. Gloucester and Edmund have died offstage.

A death march is sounded as the bodies are taken
up and the stage is cleared in a sad recession.

A STEP BEYOND

Tests and Answers

TESTS

Test 1

1. In the opening lines of the play _____
   A. Lear divides his land among his daughters
   B. Gloucester acknowledges his son, Edmund
   C. we learn why Edgar may decide to flee

2. Shakespeare frequently refers to eyesight in order to emphasize _____
   A. the violence perpetrated against Gloucester
   B. Lear's "blindness"
   C. Cordelia's vision of the future

3. The mad King Lear speaks of _____
     I. corruption in mankind
     II. man's sanctimonious qualities
     III. evil in high places
   A. I and II only
   B. I and III only
   C. I, II, and III

4. The beginning of the end for King Lear may be found in his line _____
   A. "These late eclipses in the sun and moon portend no good to us"
   B. "I prithee, daughter, do not make me mad"
   C. "Which of you shall we say doth love us most?"

5. A good example of Lear's arrogance is seen in   _____
   his statement to the loyal Kent
   A. "Mend your speech lest it may mar your
      fortune"
   B. "Come not between the dragon and his
      wrath"
   C. "If you come slack of former service, you
      shall do well"

6. "Sir, I love you more than words can wield the   _____
   matter" could not have been spoken by
   A. Regan   B. Cordelia   C. Goneril

7. The King of France urges the Duke of   _____
   Burgundy to marry Cordelia, saying
   A. "Take her or leave her"
   B. "She is herself a dowry"
   C. "No vicious blot deprived her of favour"

8. Shortly after Regan and Goneril publicly   _____
   professed their love for their father
   A. they criticized him privately
   B. they made plans to destroy Cordelia
   C. they denied him access to their castles

9. Edmund resents   _____
   A. his illegitimacy
   B. having been rejected by his father
   C. his lack of opportunity for advancement

10. Gloucester resembles Lear in that he   _____
    A. turns a deaf ear to those who can help
       him
    B. moves too rashly against his child
    C. is willing to risk his life for what he believes
       in

11. In Act II, Scene ii, the disguised Kent draws his sword
    on Oswald and attempts to engage him in a duel. The
    cowardly Oswald backs off, fearing that he will be mur-

dered. If they had not been interrupted by the party
from within the castle, would Kent have slain Oswald?
How would he justify it? If not, why?

12. Since Albany is painted in such virtuous colors and
behaves so nobly throughout the play, why doesn't he
take over the rule of the entire country at the end? Why
does he pass it on?

13. Three great villains—Cornwall, Regan, and Goneril—
die offstage. Only Edmund, their equal in villainy, and
Oswald, a "subvillain," are slain in front of the audience. How do you account for this? Why don't we witness all the villains getting their punishment? Does it
make any difference?

14. Do you think Edgar would make a good king of
England? Why?

15. Was Shakespeare secretly "antimonarchist"?

Test 2

1. In his striving for power, possessions, and   _____
women, Edmund may best be described as a
   A. ruthless materialist
   B. Machiavellian villain
   C. rank Philistine

2. Edmund detests his brother and his father for   _____
their
   A. lack of imagination
   B. credulity
   C. social graces and respectability

3. It is ironic that   _____
   I. Old Lear is treated as a child by his
      daughters
   II. loyal Kent was banished by Lear
   III. Gloucester doesn't see straight until he
      is blinded

A. I and II only
B. I and III only
C. I, II, and III

4. Kent had been placed in the stocks because _____
   A. he assaulted Goneril's servant
   B. his blunt talk outraged Lear
   C. Regan and Cornwall wanted to make an
      example of him

5. The Fool's enigmatic last line in this play is _____
   A. "And I'll go to bed at noon"
   B. "Pour on. I will endure"
   C. "Away! the foul fiend follows me!"

6. Although Lear is furious when not shown _____
   proper respect
   A. he is powerless to act against Cordelia's
      impudence
   B. he is willing to be shown the error of his
      ways
   C. he allows the Fool to criticize him

7. When Lear is frustrated by Goneril, he _____
   A. places a terrible curse on her
   B. appeals to her husband
   C. asks for forgiveness of Cordelia

8. In the quest for Edmund's love _____
   A. both sisters are willing to renounce their
      husbands
   B. Goneril poisons Regan
   C. Regan endangers Cornwall's life

9. In reply to Lear's pitiful complaint, "I gave _____
   you all," Regan replies
   A. "And in good time you gave it!"
   B. "I pray you, father, being weak, seem
      so"
   C. "How sharper than a serpent's tooth it is
      To have a thankless father"

10. The terrible storm upon the heath   ———
    A. was forecast accurately by Lear's Fool
    B. leads to Edgar's insanity as well
    C. parallels the storm within Lear

11. What is the position of women as presented in *King Lear*?

12. Without a vast stage to sweep across, how does Shakespeare show the sense of urgency and forward motion we feel throughout the play?

13. Is it fair to attribute Goneril's and Regan's behavior to greed?

14. Is there a difference between the father-daughter relationships and the father-son relationships in the play? If so, how is it shown?

15. Do Lear's daughters represent separate fragments of his own character and personality?

ANSWERS

Test 1

1. B   2. B   3. C   4. C   5. B   6. B
7. B   8. A   9. A   10. B

    11.   Does the tone of Kent's badgering suggest that he really intends to commit murder? Doesn't the scene have comedic overtones, especially Kent's description of Oswald? Kent has a firm sense of justice. Listen to what he says when he tries to convince Lear that banishment of Cordelia is wrong. Even when he is introduced to the bastard, Edmund, he is the soul of propriety.

    On the other hand, Oswald is allied with Goneril, whom Kent has seen taunting and abusing Lear. The handwriting is on the wall. In his defense to Cornwall, Kent certainly talks boldly about doing away with Oswald. Perhaps this would have kept Goneril's message from being delivered and the course of the play would have taken a different turn.

12.   Albany has claimed that his fight with France is for the restoration of Lear's rights; it is not a war over property. Would we regard him so highly if he suddenly decided that he now had a right to take over everything? Go back over what Albany has to say at various times and you will see that greed has never been a part of his character. You'll also discover other reasons to support his final position.

Consider, too, Albany as a reprentative of one faction; that is, the North. Wouldn't the threatened civil war erupt in earnest if he placed himself on the throne?

13.   Despite the explicit horror of the blinding scene, Shakespeare was not particularly interested in presenting gory details on stage. People were killed only when their death moved the action of the drama forward.

How would the audience feel if Cornwall died immediately after blinding Gloucester? Wouldn't our desire for revenge be satisfied a bit too soon? And what about the impact of the other deaths occurring in the final scene? Wouldn't they be lessened by an ongoing scene of expirations?

Consider the balance Shakespeare achieved in disposing of his villains. And consider their punishments vis-à-vis their crimes.

14.   To evaluate Edgar's qualifications, you have to consider not only his own development but the errors of his predecessor. Review the balance of their behavior and you will find definite signs of character that may be proper or may be problems for Edgar. Within the text of the play there is enough material to develop a projected character sketch for Edgar, which should guide your answer.

15.   There are two angles to consider. The first is obviously your view of his attitude toward Lear as king. That he pointed out Lear's failures is certain. But how does he balance them with Lear's redeeming qualities? And are they necessarily the failures of a king, or of a man?

The other view is the more general picture of "rulers" that comes up here and there throughout the play. It is more subtle but still applies to the question. This includes the final decision to leave Edgar in charge. Will he be a worthy successor?

Test 2

1. A **2.** B **3.** C **4.** A **5.** A **6.** C
7. A **8.** B **9.** A **10.** C

11. It's fairly safe to assume that Shakespeare reflected the views of his time. There's little suggestion of prehistoric England, despite the general setting. But without going to outside references, a picture may be developed from the play itself.

Women are presented as both daughters and wives, and there are only three of them—Goneril, Regan, and Cordelia. That in itself tells us that it's essentially a man's world. But women do not lack power. As you review their relationships and their comments, you will develop a broader understanding of women in the "natural order," too, which was one of Shakespeare's concerns.

12. There are references at the start of several scenes that indicate a passage of time. Review them and you will discover the chronological length of time that passes in the course of the action.

Just as important is the image of a journey taken by the focal characters of the main and subplots. The discussion of movement and travel helps sustain the momentum. And, of course, the constant entrances and exits as the only way of beginning and ending scenes should be considered.

13. There are many reasons for their behavior, and greed is certainly one of them. When rumors are reported of differences growing between Albany and Cornwall *(III, i)*, the reason given is the desire to control the entire kingdom. But what we know of Albany makes us suspect that it is

Goneril, rather than her husband, who is behind the rumor.

Consider, too, the confrontation scene with Lear. More than a desire to be rid of the burden of accommodating his retinue, isn't the desire for power over him a kind of greed?

And, in their wanting Edmund, doesn't the ultimate greed lead to their final destiny? As you review their moves throughout the play, you'll discover that greed plays an important part.

14. Overall, the point being made is broader than one of gender. But there are differences.

The laws of inheritance come into play here. Lear bequeaths his kingdom specifically to his daughters, but Gloucester's estate would go without question to his first-born male heir.

For the sake of parallels, however, most of the thematic concern is with children in general. It is more than a matter of verse, which puts the stress where it is in Lear's observation:

> How sharper than a serpent's tooth it is
> To have a thankless child.
> *(Act I, Scene iv, lines 279-80.)*

Consider the comments made by both fathers, as well as others, and a case may be made for both the specific and general views.

15. Lear displays an incredible number of sides in the course of this play. If you extract certain traits, you can see them appear in one daughter or another.

For example, he is obviously stubborn. But in the very first scene, Cordelia is easily his match in holding on to a position once it is taken.

His concern for quantity over quality is shown by the contest he sets up between the three daughters: "How much do you love me?" Goneril and Regan hurl quantity at him in Act II, Scene iv, when they ask why he needs so many knights.

There are many such parallels. You must decide if they add up to a complete personality or are mere chips off the paternal block.

Term Paper Ideas

1. **ANIMAL IMAGERY:** Discuss the references to animals that abound throughout the play. What do they tell us about the character speaking as well as the character spoken of?

2. **PAIN:** Pain plays an important part in *King Lear*. Consider it from the angles of those who suffer as well as those who inflict.

3. **SACRIFICE:** What sacrifices are made? By whom? For what purpose?

4. **ADULTERY:** Discuss the viewpoints expounded by various characters and the attitude of the playwright.

5. **ROMANCE:** There are passionate relationships between men and women in this play, but is there "romance"? Do Shakespeare's characters live in a world without romantic love?

6. **HEALING:** There are two types of wounds with which to deal—physical and mental. Discuss the actual examples as well as the broader concerns of the healing powers.

7. **FRANCE:** The King of France disappears as a character after the first scene, but the emblem of the country figures in the solution. Discuss.

8. ANACHRONISMS: Do they interfere with our acceptance of the events taking place? Are there many? Are they important?

9. LETTERS: There are so many letters and messages sent that they seem more important than some characters on stage. Discuss.

10. MUSIC: Discuss the function of music as it's used to create settings and relate offstage action.

11. PATRIOTISM: Reaction to the French invasion is one indication. Are there any other indicators of a concern for the country?

12. CLOTHING: Clothing makes the man or woman; nakedness does the opposite. Discuss.

13. MADNESS: We are told that there is "Reason in madness" *(IV, vi, 172).* How true is this?

14. FIDELITY: Fidelity to a master and fidelity in marriage are examined through various relationships. Discuss.

15. PRIDE: A sense of pride can be a force for good or evil. Discuss.

16. RETIREMENT: There is more than one view. Discuss the pros and cons.

17. REVENGE: It seems to be a great motivation but is it a great factor in the play? Discuss its importance.

18. THE COSMOS: Many references to the heavens, gods, planets, and so on, occur. What do they reveal about the various characters?

19. SUICIDE: Discuss Shakespeare's attitude toward suicide from what different characters say and do in *King Lear.*

20. THE STORM: Discuss its function in the play.

21. SUPERSTITION: Omens, charms, symbols—what role have they in this play?

22. CORPORAL PUNISHMENT: The use of the stocks is one example, but other characters are struck, and so on. Discuss its relevance to the larger themes.

Further Reading

CRITICAL WORKS

Bradley, A. C. *Shakespearean Tragedy*. New York: Ballantine Books, 1983, pp. 200–74.

Brooke, Tucker. "*King Lear* on Stage," in *Essays on Shakespeare*. New Haven: Archon Books, 1969, pp. 57–70.

Danby, John. *Shakespeare's Doctrine of Nature, A Study of King Lear*. London: Faber & Faber, 1964.

French, Marilyn. *Shakespeare's Division of Experience*. New York: Ballantine, 1983.

Goddard, Harold C. *The Meaning of Shakespeare*, vol. 2. Chicago: University of Chicago Press, 1951, pp. 136–71.

Granville-Barker, Harley. *Prefaces to Shakespeare*, vol. 1. Princeton: Princeton University Press, 1978, pp. 261–334.

Harbage, Alfred, ed. *Shakespeare, The Tragedies*. Englewood Cliffs, N.J.: Prentice-Hall, 1964, pp. 113–47.

Knight, G. Wilson. *The Wheel of Fire*. New York: Meridian Books, 1962, chaps. 8 and 9.

Rackin, Phyllis. *Shakespeare's Tragedies*. New York: Frederick Ungar, 1978, pp. 86–106.

Rowse, A. L. *Shakespeare, A Biography*. New York: Harper & Row, 1963.

Traversi, D. A. *An Approach to Shakespeare*. New York: Doubleday, 1969.

Van Doren, Mark. *Shakespeare*. New York: Henry Holt, 1939, pp. 238–51.

Webster, Margaret. *Shakespeare Without Tears*, New York. World Publishing Company, 1955.

AUTHOR'S OTHER WORKS

Shakespeare wrote 37 plays (38 if you include *The Two Noble Kinsmen*) over a 20-year period, from about 1590 to 1610. It's difficult to determine the exact dates when many were written, but scholars have made the following intelligent guesses about his plays and poems:

Plays

1588–93	*The Comedy of Errors*
1588–94	*Love's Labor's Lost*
1590–91	*2 Henry VI*
1590–91	*3 Henry VI*
1591–92	*1 Henry VI*
1592–93	*Richard III*
1592–94	*Titus Andronicus*
1593–94	*The Taming of the Shrew*
1593–95	*The Two Gentlemen of Verona*
1594–96	*Romeo and Juliet*
1595	*Richard II*
1594–96	*A Midsummer Night's Dream*
1596–97	*King John*
1596–97	*The Merchant of Venice*
1597	*1 Henry IV*
1597–98	*2 Henry IV*
1598–99	*Henry V*
1598–1600	*Much Ado About Nothing*
1599	*Julius Caesar*
1599–1600	*As You Like It*
1599–1600	*Twelfth Night*
1600–01	*Hamlet*
1597–1601	*The Merry Wives of Windsor*
1601–02	*Troilus and Cressida*
1602–04	*All's Well That Ends Well*

Glossary

There are many unfamiliar terms, words, and phrases in *King Lear*, most of which can be understood from the context in which they appear. Some recur frequently and seem strange only because of usage. Here are a few that have slightly different meanings from our present usage.

Whoreson, Bastard, Base These were not necessarily curses. They were commonly used to describe the origins of birth. Sometimes the reference to low birth carried a sting, too.

Fortune A holdover from the Middle Ages, the image of the Wheel of Fortune was a strong one. It was seen to be the barometer of man's fate that turned constantly, moving the bottom to the top and vice versa.

Villain, Villainy   Our present-day equivalent would probably be *criminal* and *crime*. There were varying degrees,
from an affectionate use to actual accusation of wrongdo-
ing. Again, reading the word in context will provide a
clue to the vehemence intended.

Treachery, Traitor   Any form of betrayal was treachery
and the perpetrator was a traitor. From the common tat-
tletale to the commission of major crime of betrayal, the
words were commonly applied.

Monster   Another relic of the Middle Ages that Shakespeare and his contemporaries commonly incorporated
into their routine philosophy. The personification of disorder was the monster. An upset or inversion of the
ordered world, the benign forces, was the monstrous, the
chaotic. Grotesque images were frequently used to represent this manifestation of evil and disorder.

Wit   Wit was more than cleverness. Wit represented the
human intelligence, the ability to reason. When someone
lost his reason, his sanity, he lost his wits. At times it also
indicated cunning and the ability to exploit words to a
greater purpose.

The Critics

The Message of *King Lear*

. . . the theme of King Lear may be stated in psycho-
logical as well as biological terms. So put, it is the
destructive, the ultimately suicidal character of unreg-
ulated passion, its power to carry human nature back to
chaos. . . .

The predestined end of unmastered passion is the
suicide of the species. That is the gospel according to
King Lear. The play is in no small measure an actual
representation of that process. The murder-suicide of
Regan-Goneril is an example. But it is more than a pic-

ture of chaos and impending doom. What is the remedy for chaos? it asks. What can avert the doom? The characters who have mastered their passions give us a glimpse of the answer to those questions.

—*Harold C. Goddard*, The Meaning of Shakespeare, *1951*

On Lear

The initial act of the hero is his only act; the remainder is passion. An old and weary king, hungry for rest, banishes the one daughter who would give it to him and plunges at once into the long, loud night of his catastrophe. An early recognition of his error does not save him. The poet does not wish to save him, for his instinct is to develop a catastrophe as none has been developed before or since.

—*Mark Van Doren*, Shakespeare, *1939*

Lear's progress—dramatic and spiritual—lies through a dissipation of egoism; submission to the cruelty of an indifferent Nature, less cruel to him than are his own kin; to ultimate loss of himself in madness.

—*Harley Granville-Barker*, Prefaces to Shakespeare, *1946*

The Secondary Plot

The secondary plot fills out a story which would by itself have been somewhat thin, and it provides a most effective contrast between its personages and those of the main plot, the tragic strength and stature being heightened by comparison with the slighter build of the former.

—*A. C. Bradley*, Shakespearean Tragedy, *1983*

. . . the subplot simplifies the central action, translating its concerns into familiar (and therefore easily apprehensible) verbal and visual patterns. The subplot is easier to grasp because its characters tend to account for their sufferings in traditional moral language; it also